THE USS GAMBLE IN
THE SOUTH PACIFIC
WORLD WAR TWO

THE USS GAMBLE IN THE SOUTH PACIFIC
WORLD WAR TWO

Written and Compiled by Richard Hansen

with a Forward by C. G. Smith

SOLVING LIGHT BOOKS
727 MOUNT ALBAN DRIVE
ANNAPOLIS, MD 21409
solvinglight.com

ISBN - 13: 978-0692260135

ISBN - 10: 0692260137

Acknowledgements

Thanks to Bella's Liquors in the Cape St. Claire Shopping Center, Annapolis, Maryland for financing the production of this book, and to Bob Johnson of Solving Light Books for producing it.

Dedication

To the unsung heros of World War Two, the men who served on our ships, many of whom sacrificed their lives at sea in order to protect our navy and our nation.

These men did not ask for honor or special favors; they were just doing their jobs. Our dad was one of these unsung heros.

We hope you enjoy reading about the *USS Gamble* and the other ships mentioned herein whose dedicated and courageous crews played a crucial part in defending our liberty and avenging the Japanese attack on Pearl Harbor.

The Smith Kids

Forward by C. G. Smith

Interesting that I learned the USS GAMBLE DD-123 was first commissioned 19 November, 1918 in Norfolk, Virginia because my birthday is that very same date. Fate had something in store for us both.

Due to the new federal draft, I enlisted in the Navy for four years in February, 1941. As a 22-year-old, I was eager to go to sea. I had great expectations of boarding a ship and "joining the Navy to see the world." Things happened sooner than I anticipated. Two days after taking the oath, twenty raw recruits and yours truly were hustled together for our first voyage, embarking from New York to Newport, Rhode Island on a ferry boat for training. It was boot camp, a stint of school in San Diego, and off to Hawaii for fleet assignment. Mine was the GAMBLE, and she would be my home for two and a half years.

That is how I got there, but the main story is the important operations of the GAMBLE and her history so thoroughly explored and presented in this book. This history highlights the unsung accomplishments of the GAMBLE and ships like her whose activities helped secure the entire South Pacific during World War Two.

My family and I decided to honor this gallant old ship with this story about her. Memory at my age is vague but I had a lot of documents and data that had been compiled by Richard Hansen, a crew member. With this data and the work of Solving Light Books, we have an accurate portrayal of the GAMBLE's wartime activity.

I hope that my family for generations to come will read this and realize that "Pops" was part of the GAMBLE crew from Pearl Harbor to almost the war's end—a long haul.

The GAMBLE went on without me until her last battle at Iwo Jima where bombs rendered her unfit for duty. I know that if there are any remaining members of the fine crews that manned her, they will all salute the USS GAMBLE DD-123/DM-15. She rests at the bottom of the sea off Apra Harbor, Guam.

USS GAMBLE

FIRST COMMISSIONED as DD-123, 19 November, 1918, Norfolk, Virginia

DECOMMISSIONED, 17 June, 1922, SAN DIEGO, CALIFORNIA

RECOMMISSIONED, 24 May, 1930 and reclassified as DM-15.

DECOMMISSIONED 22 December, 1937, San Diego, California

RECOMMISSIONED 25 September, 1939 San Diego, California,

NEW NUMBERS INSTALLED ABOUT 5 October, 1939 as DM-15

CHANGED TO A "THREE STACKER" August, 1943

Table of Contents

COMMANDING OFFICERS OF USS GAMBLE (DM 15)

September 25, 1939 to September, 1940 — Smith, Allen E, Cmdr., USN
September, 1940 to 8 February, 1942 — Crandell, D.A., Lt., USN
8 February, 1942 to 15 April, 1942 — Brown, E.M., Lt. USN
15 April, 1942 to 3 March, 1943 — Tackney, S.N., Lt. Cmdr., USN
3 March, 1943 to 25 July, 1944 — Armstrong, Warren W., LCDR, USN
25 July, 1944 to 28 February, 1945 — Clay, D.N., Lt. LCDR, USN
28 February, 1945 to 1 June, 1945 — Peterson, R.J., Lt. USNR

EXECUTIVE OFFICERS

September, 1939 to December, 1941 — Brown, E.M., Lt., USN
December, 1941 to October, 1942 — Smith, Millard J., Lt. USN
October, 1942 to July, 1943 — Goodloe, G. C., Lt. USNR
August, 1943 to October, 1944 — Carpenter, R.E., Lt. USNR
November, 1944 to February, 1945 — Peterson, R. J., Lt., USNR
February, 1945 to 1 June, 1945 — Stewart, E.R., Lt. USNR

NUMBER OF ENLISTED PERSONNEL AT SELECTED DATES

October, 1939 — 75
December, 1939 — 98
March, 1940 — 106
June, 1940 — 103
September, 1940 — 103
December, 1940 — 122
April, 1941 — 130
July, 1941 — 128
September, 1941 — 122
December, 1941 — 130
March, 1942 — 138
June, 1942 — 120
September, 1942 — 137
December, 1942 — 128
March, 1943 — 130
June, 1943 — 127
September, 1943 — 139
December, 1943 — 138
March, 1944 — 137
June, 1944 — 129
September, 1944 — 136
December, 1944 — 137
March, 1945 — 114
June, 1945 — 0

The *Gamble* was decommissioned 1 June, 1945 and all personnel transferred to other duties.

On 16 July, 1945, She was towed outside Apra Harbor, Guam, and sunk

Short History of the USS Gamble

From the Dictionary of American Naval Fighting Ships Naval History and Heritage Command

Named jointly in honor of two brothers, heroes of the War of 1812.

Lt. Peter Gamble, was born in Bordentown, New Jersey, appointed midshipman 16 January 1809, served on Macdonough's flagship *Saratoga* in the Battle of Lake Champlain, and was killed in action while in the act of sighting his gun on 11 September 1814. Macdonough deplored his loss and commended his gallantry in action.

Lt. Col. John M. Gamble, USMC, was born in Brooklyn, New York in 1791, appointed 2d Lt. on 16 January 1809, and distinguished himself by coolness and bravery in many enterprises, including critical encounters with hostile natives of the Marquesa Islands during the absence of frigate *Essex* in 1813, and sailing a prize of *Essex,* with only a four-man crew and without benefit of a chart, in a remarkable 17-day voyage to the Hawaiian Islands. He was breveted a Lt. Col. on 3 March 1827 and died in New York 11 September 1836.

The USS GAMBLE (DD-123) was launched on 11 May 1918 by the Newport News Shipbuilding & Dry Dock Co., Newport News, Virginia, sponsored by Miss Evelyn H. Jackson, a relative of Secretary of the Navy Josephus Daniels; and commissioned at Norfolk on 19 November 1918, Comdr. H. J. Abbett in command.

After shakedown training out of the Virginia Capes, GAMBLE sailed from New York on 13 January 1919 to take part in maneuvers off Cuba, Key West, Florida, and the New England seaboard until June 1919. Following overhaul at Norfolk, she joined the Pacific Fleet at San Diego on 7 August 1919 and operated along the Pacific coast until placed in reserve status in the Mare Island Navy Yard on 1 December 1919. In October 1920, she came out of reserve and assisted the flotilla in torpedo practice, maneuvered with the Battle Force, and cruised along the California coast as a training ship for reservists. She decommissioned at San Diego 17 June 1922.

The Oiler *USS Cuyama* (largest ship) at Acapulco, Mexico, circa 1919 with destroyers alongside. From left to center: *USS Walker* (DD-163), *USS Crosby* (DD-164), *USS Thatcher* (DD-162). *USS Gamble* (DD-123) is moored along *Cuyama's* port side.
U.S. Naval Historical Center Photograph courtesy of Donald M. McPherson.

USS Gamble **with other destroyers at Mare Island Navy Yard, 1919. From left to right: *USS Tarbell* (DD-142), *USS Thatcher* (DD-162), *USS Rizal* (DD-174), *USS Hart* (DD-110), *USS Hogan* (DD-178), *USS Gamble* (DD-123), *USS Ramsay* (DD-124) and *USS Williams* (DD-108).**
Photo a Donation of Rear Admiral Ammen Farenholt, USN.

USS Gamble **Anchored and Dressed with Flags Circa. 1921**

GAMBLE, recommissioned on 24 May 1930, was reclassified (DM-15) on 13 June, and converted into a light minelayer in the Mare Island Navy Yard. Arriving at Pearl Harbor from the West Coast, she became flagship of Mine Squadron 2 in July 1930 and later served as flagship of Mine Division 1, Mine Squadron 1. She cruised Hawaiian waters instructing naval reservists in mine warfare and acted as plane guard and radio tracker for seaplanes, each year participating in fleet readiness and fleet exercises until she returned to San Diego where she was decommissioned on 22 December 1937. Recommissioned on 25 September 1939 as Europe was plunged into World War II, she joined Mine Division 5 in patrol and performed school-ship duties out of San Francisco. In April 1941, she proceeded to Pearl Harbor for war readiness patrol in Hawaiian waters as a unit of Mine Division 2.

On 7 December 1941, GAMBLE returned from offshore patrol. Japanese carrier-based planes pounding our ships in the harbor broke her peaceful Sunday morning routine. GAMBLE's gunners joined the fire of other warships and had the satisfaction of seeing one enemy plane fall into the water off her port beam. After the attack, she took an antisubmarine patrol station in the screen of the carrier ENTERPRISE (CV-6), and later guarded the approaches to Pearl Harbor. In mid-February 1942, she headed south in the escort for a convoy to Pago Pago, Samoa; then joined RAMSEY in laying a protective mine field off Tutuila. At the end of March, the two minelayers shifted to the Fiji Islands, to lay a minefield in Nandi waters from 7 - 14 April.

The U.S. Navy battleship *USS California* (BB-44) slowly sinking alongside Ford Island, Pearl Harbor, Hawaii (USA). The destroyer *USS Shaw* (DD-373) is burning in the floating dry dock YFD-2 in the left distance. The battleship *USS Nevada* (BB-36) is beached in the left-center distance.

U.S. Navy battleships at Pearl Harbor on 7 December 1941 (l-r): *USS West Virginia* (BB-48) (sunk), *USS Tennessee* (BB-43) (damaged), and the *USS Arizona* (BB-39) (sunk).

***USS Gamble* (DM-15) in late 1940 at the Golden Gate International Exposition
(Worlds Fair) at San Francisco.**

Returning to Pearl Harbor for heavier armament, GAMBLE helped safeguard convoys to Midway during the time of that crucial and historic battle, then headed south with BREESE and TRACY to lay a defensive minefield off the entrance to Second Channel, Espiritu Santo, New Hebrides Islands.

On 27 August 1942, GAMBLE joined a task unit headed to Guadalcanal. Although designated a destroyer-minelayer, the old four-piper still carried antisubmarine gear. When her lookouts spotted an enemy submarine on the morning of 29 August, she went into action. After several depth charge attacks, GAMBLE ran through large oil slicks, found deck planking, and observed a large air bubble break the surface. Later her victim was identified as Japanese submarine *I-123,* whose dying radio had signaled "under heavy enemy attack." That afternoon she proceeded at full speed to Nura Island where she rescued four stranded aviators from the aircraft carrier SARATOGA. Continuing to aid in the bitter struggle for Guadalcanal, she transported 158 marines to the island on 31 August, patrolled off Lunga Roads, then on 5 September, assisted in freeing the grounded transport WILLIAM WARD BURROWS (AP-6) and escorted her to Espiritu Santo, New Hebrides. Her patrol, escort, and transport duties continued as the drive for Guadalcanal pressed on to victory.

Five minutes after midnight, on 6 May 1943, GAMBLE, with minelayers PREBLE and BREESE turned simultaneously in rain squalls which broke at times to disclose each to the other in perfect formation. Making 15 knots, each ship dropped a mine every 12 seconds, planting over 250 mines in 17 minutes across Blackett Strait, the western entrance to Kula Gulf and directly in the favorite route of the worrisome "Tokyo Express." The ships then sped north to join the protective screen of Rear Admiral Ainsworth's cruiser-destroyer force before refueling at Tulagi. On the night of 7-8 May, four Japanese destroyers entered the mined waters. One, *Kurashio,* went down, two others, *Oyashio* and *Kagero,* were badly damaged and sent out calls for help that brought the fourth destroyer *Michishio* to the scene. Aircraft, alerted by a coast-watcher, intercepted the rescue operation, sinking the two destroyers and sending *Michishio* limping back to port, badly damaged.

On 30 June 1943, during the invasion of New Georgia, GAMBLE laid a string of mines off the beachhead, before returning to Tulagi. In July, welcome orders sent her back to the United States for overhaul. She headed west again 20 September 1943. Her minelaying duties then brought her to Empress Augusta Bay on 1-2 November 1943 to support landing operations; Bougainville Strait, 7-8 November; Purvis Bay, Florida Island, 23-24 November, thence to the New Hebrides Islands for escort duty among the Solomons until she returned to San Francisco on 12 October 1944.

After overhaul and refresher training, GAMBLE departed San Diego on 7 January 1945, en route via Hawaii and the Marshalls to Iwo Jima where she arrived 17 February, to lend fire support to the various sweeping units, and to explode floating mines. During her shelling, a direct hit on an ammunition dump exploded the enemy magazine like a giant firecracker at the foot of Mt. Surabachi.

On 18 February 1945, GAMBLE was hit just above the waterline by two 250-pound bombs. Both firerooms immediately flooded and she became dead in the water with two holes in her bottom as all hands fought raging fires, jettisoned topside weight, and shored damaged bulkheads. Five men were killed, one missing in action, and eight wounded. As marines stormed the shores of Iwo Jima the next day, GAMBLE was taken in tow by DORSEY who turned her over to *L8M-126* for passage to Saipan. She arrived at Saipan on 24 February and went alongside HAMUL for repair.

Some hope remained for GAMBLE for a long time, but on 1 June 1945 she decommissioned, and on 16 July, she was towed outside Apra Harbor, Guam, and sunk.

GAMBLE received seven battle stars for service in World War II. ⚓

OFFENSIVE MINE LAYING BY SURFACE CRAFT DURING THE SECOND WORLD WAR PACIFIC THEATRE

It took some time for the American Naval Forces to recover from the effects of the disastrous Japanese attack on Pearl Harbor but by mid-1942, enough manpower, materiel, and ships had been assembled to start the invasions that would island-hop American forces across the Pacific to eventual victory against the Japanese. The first target was the lower Solomon Islands, specifically, Guadalcanal with a newly constructed airfield, and the island of Florida with Purvis Bay and Tulagi Harbors.

On August 6, 1942 the American forces were assembled and ready to begin the long march to Tokyo. The invasion of Guadalcanal and Tulagi established a pattern that was to be repeated in every landing that occurred in the Pacific. The minesweepers led the fleet to clear a path that was almost certainly made free of enemy mines. At Guadalcanal, the first combat minesweeping by invading forces started at 1000 in the passage between Gavutu and Bungala Islands. By 1153 a total of six passes had been made through the area. No mines were found and the area was declared safe for passage, at least as far as mines were concerned. Sporadic gunfire from nearby Gavutu Island still made a safe passage uncertain though none of the sweepers were hit. The sweepers who took part in this historic sweep were the HOVEY, ZANE, SOUTHARD, HOPKINS, and TREVER, all converted from WW I destroyers.

From Top: Destroyer Minelayers *Hovey, Zane*, and *Southard.*

From top: Destroyer Minelayers *Hopkins* and *Trever*.

The next channel demanding clearance was Lunga along the coast of Guadalcanal. All the sweepers moved across the channel to participate, continuing their sweeping operations right through the landings of August 7th and on into the 8th. That's the day all hell broke loose. The Japanese were apparently offended by the audacious behavior of the American forces and sent down a large flight of twin engine bombers, probably Bettys (Mitsubishi G4Ms), with a group of Zekes (Mitsubishi A6M Zeros) for escort. Shipping was crowded in the waters off Guadalcanal and each ship took over its own destiny, zigging and zagging to avoid the bombers and fighters, as well as each other.

USS George F Elliott (AP-13), commissioned 10 January 1941. Lost to enemy action, 8 August 1942 shortly after 8 am off Guadalcanal.

The HOVEY, in the thick of everything, expended over 5,000 rounds of 50 caliber ammunition and a lot of 3" ammo before the raid was over. She was credited with two probables and certainly damaged two others. TREVER knocked down four bombers and ZANE knocked down one. All the sweepers scared a lot of other planes with near misses. The only American ship sunk during the raid was the transport GEORGE F ELLIOT, hit by a Japanese suicide plane, determined to take such drastic action. HOVEY rescued 120 survivors off the GEORGE F ELLIOTT and took them to Tulagi. The same day, HOPKINS tried to take in tow the heavy cruiser ASTORIA, badly damaged the night before in the First Battle of Savo Island, but had to release when ASTORIA blew up after fires had reached her magazine.

The same day, TRACY was laying a string of 85 mines in Marimasike Passage along the east coast of Malaita Island, just off Guadalcanal. This field produced no known results but did have its effect. It eliminated a short cut for the Japanese destroyers and kept them from at least one piece of coast occupied by the United States Marines, for which they were grateful, no doubt.

Above: *USS Hopkins* **steams past the transport area between Guadalcanal and Tulagi, 8 August 1942. Ship burning in the left distance is** *USS George F. Elliott* **(AP-13), which had been hit by a Japanese air attack earlier in the day.**
Right: The *George F. Elliot* **on fire.**

USS Astoria, **"Nasty Asty" to her crew, was originally lead ship of her class of heavy cruisers. She saw service from April 1934 through August 1942, when she was lost in night action off Guadalcanal. The** *USS Hopkins* **was unable to keep her in tow when the fires from the attack reached her magazine.**

For the next several months, a few high-speed minelayers and sweepers were the first line of defense for American forces in the Solomons. After the third Battle of Savo Island, most other American naval ships were withdrawn from the area to avoid risk of their encountering a larger Japanese force in restrictive waters. The few old four stacker minesweepers and minelayers weren't much of a force against the might of the Japanese navy, and they certainly didn't go out looking for trouble, but by their very presence made some show of force. And they were effective.

The Destroyer Minelayer
***USS Gamble* photographed**
in December, 1944

For the Destroyer/Minelayer GAMBLE, August 24, 1942 was a banner day. On that day her skipper, Lieutenant Commander Tackney earned a Navy Cross and her crew had the satisfaction of knowing that they earned their keep. On her way to assist in the defense of Guadalcanal, one of her lookouts, early in the 0800 to 1200 watch, spotted what appeared to be an enemy submarine at a distance of about 10,000 yards. Only a fluke had taken the GAMBLE into the position she was in when the submarine was spotted. GAMBLE had received a radio message that four or five aviators from the carrier SARATOGA were ashore on tiny Nura Island near San Christoval. GAMBLE had moved to within a few thousand yards and launched her whale boat to rescue the flyers. Don Hoffman, Coxswain, took the regular crew and a few spare hands to make the rescue, figuring they would probably have to swim to shore over the reef to rescue the flyers. The trip took a lot longer than he had bargained on because he had no sooner cleared the ship than the submarine was sighted.

As soon as it was sighted, the sub dove, and the GAMBLE took off in hot pursuit, her sonar pinging away, and the entire crew at general quarters. Three times the GAMBLE passed over the sub's supposed location and each time she laid a nice string of depth charges that exploded at various depths. On the third pass, oil, deck planking, and other debris floated to the surface signifying the apparent end of the submarine. The GAMBLE was credited with the sub's destruction, and this was confirmed by Japanese sources after the war. Now coincidence, almost beyond belief, asserted itself.

During her successful attack on Japanese submarine 1-123, crew members of the *Gamble* rescued four or five pilots from the *USS Saratoga*, pictured above, stranded on tiny Nura Island. The photo was taken from one of her planes of Carrier Air Group 12 (CVG-12), of which many aircraft are visible on deck: Douglas SBD Dauntless dive bombers (aft), Grumman F6F Hellcat fighters (mostly forward), and Grumman TBF Avenger torpedo bombers.

The Japanese submarine's number was 1-123, the same number GAMBLE carried before she was converted to a minelayer. Also the 1-123 had been built as a minelaying submarine so both attacker and attackee were in the same line of work. The 1-123 was also one of the submarines that had been sent to French Frigate Shoals to refuel the Emilys (Kawanishi H8K Imperial Japanese flying boats) that made the second but inconsequential attack on Pearl Harbor on 4 March, 1942. Revenge is so sweet. Lieutenant Commander Tackney praised the crew for an excellent job. For the sonar man operating the sonar gear and the officers plotting the information and directing the attack, it was a delightful way to start a day. Oh yes! Coxswain Hoffman and the whale boat: They got the American pilots off Nura Island without incident and were back on board a little after lunch.

This wasn't the only submarine sunk by the mine force in those waters during the latter half of 1942. The SOUTHARD found another on November 10th. After a long series of search and attack maneuvers, the submarine surfaced just long enough for the crew of the 4" gun on the galley deck house to get a round through her conning tower. That finished off the Japanese Submarine 1-172.

Long before the invasion of Guadalcanal, the senior staff members of the navy had decided to make a concerted effort of offensive mine laying against the Japanese. The entire Western Pacific was considered fair game. Any method of getting the mines to their destination was considered acceptable. This included surface vessels, submarines, and aircraft. If guiding the mines into place with frogmen had been considered practical, they probably would have suggested that approach too.

Mark VI Sea Mines

The manufacture of the newly-designed mines created by Naval Ordnance Laboratory had not yet reached the point where they could be delivered to the Pacific Theatre, so the mines laid in the first year-and-a-half of the war were primarily mines left over from the North Sea Mine Barrage in WWI. These were the familiar old Mark VI mines with the little float on top that greatly increased their depth range. They were quite effective as we shall see. Moved by train from depots on the east coast they were first shipped to the mine depot at West Loch in Pearl Harbor. Here they were checked and then placed directly on surface minelayers or shipped by merchant ship to safe harbors near their point of use.

We should now stop for a moment and consider the geography of the area where offensive mines were first used in the Pacific. The Solomon Islands, first discovered by Captain Bougainville, an English explorer in the 17th century, had been under British mandate or control ever since. A few of the natives had been somewhat civilized but there were still savage tribes inhabiting some of the islands. Some were antisocial to the point of practicing cannibalism. The Solomons are a chain of volcanic islands running in a northwest, southeast direction, and are so situated so as to provide a long channel between the islands through which the Japanese navy steamed with little resistance any time they chose to make the effort. This came to be known by the sailors who guarded the shipping of Guadalcanal and the marines and soldiers who fought so fiercely on the beaches and in the jungle as "The Slot."

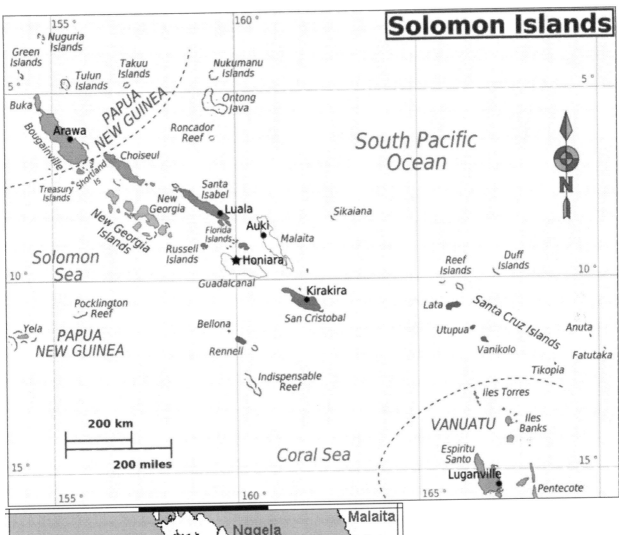

Solomon Islands

Solomon Islands with Inset of Guadalcanal

The Japanese still had control of all the islands north and east of Guadalcanal and had established army garrisons, air fields, and naval bases in protected harbors. They were hard to root out although the Cactus Air Force based at Henderson Field on Guadalcanal did a remarkable job taking on the Japanese bombers and fighters that came down to strafe and bomb the island and the shipping. The Japanese navy had an almost free hand when it came to sending down destroyers, cruisers, and battleships at night to bombard the American positions ashore. Supplies for the Japanese troops still ashore at Guadalcanal were also sneaked through the patrols in the dark of the night.

The names of the islands making up the Solomon Islands were to become household words for the men of the minelayers during the coming year-and-a-half. Names such as New Georgia, Vella Lavella, Shortland, Munda, Ferguson Passage, Kulambangara, all would see the passage of American minelayers in the months to come.

For the few American naval vessels that remained in the area after the Battle of the Eastern Solomons on August 24 and the three Battles of Savo Island, it was a nervous situation. The old minelayers assumed many duties for which they were neither designed nor outfitted. They transported the Marines to lonely beaches behind enemy lines. They acted as escort vessels for the supply ships and stood picket-line duty to warn of approaching Japanese ships or planes.

The GAMBLE was used as a tug at Tulagi to help the WILLIAM WARD BURROWS (AO-6) free herself from a reef near the entrance. After two days of throwing cargo over the side to lighten ship, the BURROWS was finally freed from the reef's grip. But that was just a temporary accommodation. Backing down at full power as she struggled to free herself while under tow from the GAMBLE, she was unable to reverse engines fast enough after getting free to avoid another reef on the other side of the channel. The GAMBLE sailors were somewhat disgusted and BURROW's skipper was humbled, but the GAMBLE stuck around and got her free again.

For most of the minecraft at that time, supplies were not only short, they were non-existent. When the minecraft had left Pearl Harbor, the sailors were assured they would be gone for a few weeks at most and would shortly return to Pearl Harbor for more supplies. Believing this, many of the ships had given away supplies to various Marine units that were also short of food. As it worked out, no supplies were forthcoming for the minecraft until December of 1942 when a couple of converted tuna boats operating out of

The *Gamble* pulled the transport *William Ward Burrows*, above, off a reef at Tulagi.

New Zealand managed to find the minecraft in various ports from Noumea to Tulagi. The GAMBLE received her supplies while anchored in Segund Channel at Espiritu Santos. It was a happy occasion for the starving sailors but the tuna boat skipper almost gave some of the crew members heart attacks before they discovered who she was. It seems the skipper of the supply boat couldn't find the GAMBLE at the anchorage in the dark and turned on her search light to get a fix on her target. The GAMBLE sailors who were topside were caught in the glare of a 24" carbon arc light. The Officer of the Day sounded general quarters and within moments, the GAMBLE was prepared to sink the invading vessel. Cooler heads prevailed, a signal was passed to the "light vessel" and she killed her light and came along side. A happy crew welcomed them even though they had almost scared the wits out of the minelayer.

All the ships, at one time or another, had a chance to send shore parties to various islands to scrounge for food and ships on off-shore patrol, cruising at only a few knots, almost always had a fishing line streaming astern with a feathered jig to attract tuna and dolphin and once in a while a barracuda. All were excellent eating and a fine supplement to the boring diet of dehydrated food. The cooks did a tremendous job with what they had to work with, but even a dedicated chef can only do so much with dehydrated cabbage and potatoes.

The GAMBLE found a goldmine of fresh supplies when she first went to Segund Channel. Her shore party not only found oranges and tangerines in abundance but also bananas for cooking, coconuts, and a live pig, furnished by a kindly plantation owner. But the biggest surprise and the most welcome item was a basket containing about 6 dozen eggs, more or less fresh which were prepared by the ship's cook as soon as the party returned. For some reason they didn't share this bonanza with the rest of the crew. The pig was butchered by a GM named Toth from Nebraska and a fine feast was had by the entire crew.

During the fall of 1942 the minecraft still in the area did a lot of boring detail work such as escorting supply ships from place to place, off-shore patrol at Segund Channel and Efate, and hunting for Japanese submarines that were known to be in the area. The sonar gear ran almost continuously for most of the ships. A few got down to Noumea for a day or two some time during the fall but visits were rare and always short. Noumea was a somewhat civilized port and did have a couple of bars, a city park, and a church built entirely of wood with not a single nail. That about ends the attractive features of Noumea except for the pink house on the hill. We won't go into detail about it even though it was a popular spot for a lot of the sailors who found themselves with a spare hour or two in town. The line was up to a mile long and carefully controlled by MPs who saw to it no one cut in.

Noumea was nothing compared to Sydney, Brisbane or Auckland, but it was better than nothing and certainly a great improvement on the beaches and rivers of the Hebrides or the Solomons. Most maintenance work on these ships was done by the crew members themselves since there were no repair ships or facilities in the area at that time. It was often difficult, if not impossible to obtain spare parts or even tools. One took very good care of what one had since there was no nearby hardware store where one could go to get new tools or anything else.

Fresh water was always at a premium. The evaporators were old, corroded, and subject to constant break down. The GAMBLE, on one memorable occasion, had to lay in Tulagi for two days and haul water from a spring in five gallon jerry cans to get enough to fill her tanks so she could get under way. Imagine, if you can, using a Higgins Boat, a couple of hundred five gallon cans, a goodly crew of men, and a climb up a slippery jungle trail to fill a 50,000 gallon fresh water tank. By the time the job was done, the evaporators were repaired but it took a good while to fill the other tank. The crew took all this in stride as just another inconvenience of fighting a war far from home waters. And of course it did give them a chance to get off the ship.

There were no more mine plants during 1942, but by 1943 plans were made to start an aggressive campaign by surface and air. Not all the mines planted were American. On February 22, 1943 Liberator bombers of the Tenth Air Force dropped British made magnetic mines in the mouth of the Rangoon River in Burma, flying out of Australian airfields. The pilots thought this was a sneaky way to fight a war. They were more used to dropping bombs and seeing immediate results or non-results of their actions. Though there was no crash of exploding bombs when they dropped their deadly cargo, they were just as deadly, and maybe more so. This first aerial mine-laying expedition was just a small sampling of what would follow during the rest of the war. In time, aerial mine-laying became the dominant method of delivery. Over the course of the war, thousands and thousands of mines were dropped from American aircraft in Japanese controlled waters, both at home and in distant ports.

The first aerial mine-laying in the Southwest Pacific was around Bougainville and was aimed at breaking the supply line which kept the Japanese bases at Buin-Kahila operating. While submarine mine-laying had been going on ever since the war started, mostly in Japanese home waters, this was the beginning of a planned offensive that would materially change Japanese shipping patterns.

Although the submarine laid minefields that were few in number, only 36 separate fields in the outer zone, the effect was remarkably productive. In those few scattered fields the submarines placed 658 mines in 33 sorties but they sank over 27 ships and damaged a number at least equal to those that were sunk. But more than that, these fields forced the Japanese to rethink their methods of supply. Many ports in Southeast Asia were simply abandoned as major shipping points. This required the Japanese to off-load from merchant ships to small junks that could navigate the unmined shallow waters. It also diverted the convoy routes to deeper waters where they were easier prey to other submarines who could sink them with torpedoes or gunfire.

By early 1943 a strong and aggressive mine-laying campaign was begun by surface craft, primarily the DMs that had been converted from WWI destroyers. They were ideal for the job since they had the speed to make runs of 300 miles or so into enemy territory,

30

Japanese troops load onto a warship in preparation for a "Tokyo Express" run sometime in 1942. The Tokyo Express was the name given by Allied forces to the use of Imperial Japanese Navy ships at night to deliver personnel, supplies, and equipment to Japanese forces operating in and around New Guinea and the Solomon Islands. The operation involved loading personnel or supplies aboard fast warships, mainly destroyers and later submarines, and using the warships' speed to deliver the personnel or supplies to the desired location and return to the originating base within one night so Allied aircraft could not intercept them by day.

most of the time under cover of darkness. Between February of 1943 and May of 1944, DMs with some help from a couple of light cruisers late in the campaign, laid 2,817 moored contact mines and 12 magnetic ground mines in 17 offensive mine fields in the Southwest Pacific. These fields claimed at least 8 vessels sunk and 3 more damaged. Not a bad return on the investment. In addition, a number of submarines were unaccounted for in the same area as the mine fields and were probable victims. Many of the fields were laid in conjunction with other tactical operations as we shall see.

It was on February 1, 1943, that the TRACY, GAMBLE, and PREBLE headed north to lay a field that everyone hoped would come as a shock to the Tokyo Express. They had loaded mines the day before at Noumea and were headed for Doma Reef, a shoal area between New Georgia and Santa Isabel Islands. This was the path generally taken by the Express and it was hoped they would find Japanese targets. The Japanese naval forces almost dominated these waters. They were particularly adept at navigating the channels in the blackest of weather. The Japanese ground forces left on Guadalcanal were not doing too well and had been all but pushed back into the sea. They were still being supplied by destroyers who ran down the "Slot" protected by other Japanese warships. It was the objective of this mine plant to stop, or at least slow down, this supply line.

A few hours before the scheduled plant the group received word that the Tokyo Express was once again on its way down The Slot, friendly snoopers had spotted them as they entered the channel, reporting that there were "a whole bunch" of them. As it developed, there were fourteen of them, all destroyers and cruisers: a formidable batch of firepower if they should catch the poorly armed minelayers. According to calculations, the Express would reach the planting area about the same time as the TRACY and her group were scheduled to begin their planting run. The Division Commander of MINDIV ONE, Lieutenant Commander J. L. Collis, also skipper of the TRACY, ordered all ships to proceed at flank speed. That meant 26 knots, a bit of a chore for the old four-stackers on a sustained run, but with the galley range cut in, it was possible with a little to spare. By 1900 hours the little group was charging through Lengo Channel off the south end of Guadalcanal. All the other American ships in the area, transports, freighters, and small craft, were heading in the other direction. But MINDIV ONE maintained its course.

By now, darkness had settled in and with it came a series of line squalls that made it impossible to see from ship to ship. Lightning blazed down from the fronts, rain fell in buckets, and the wind howled. Still the four-stackers plowed on. At 2000 hours, the little line of ships were in range of Japanese shore batteries on Guadalcanal, and it seemed they were seen by the gunners. A few rounds were fired in their general direction but none made contact.

The minelayers held their fire to avoid giving away their positions and sped on. Six miles away was Savo Island, just off the TRACY's bow, so to speak. Already a PT Boat had been found by the Japanese and set on fire with tracers, and the Japanese ships were circling about this with their searchlights on, trying to find some survivors to shoot. The TRACY and her ships sped on, ignoring the fighting off to starboard.

At 2021 hours, the TRACY gave the order to slow to 15 knots and a few moments later to execute the turn that would place them in position to start laying mines. By 2035 hours, all the mines were in the water and the TRACY's job was done. Over towards Savo Island, the PT Boats were still slugging it out with the Japanese navy. PTs 37, 311, and 123 would not return to base that night.

The original plan was for the MINDIV ONE to retire out past Cape Esperance after the mine planting was completed. Unfortunately, that route was then blocked by the rampaging Tokyo Express. It seemed there were Japanese ships everywhere. In fact, they were less than 12,000 yards distant and closing fast. Lt Cmdr Collis believed discretion was the better part of valor and executed that old navy trick known as "getting the hell out of there." After all, they had done their assigned task and there was little point in challenging a substantial portion of the Japanese navy with the fire power they had. So the little group made a 180-degree turn and headed back down Lengo Channel.

Just to be on the safe side, Collis broke radio silence and told the other American ships in the area what he was doing. There was no point in letting his little group be mistaken for Japanese. At 2140 hours, more bad news came over the TBS. Henderson Field advised him that there was a large group of Japanese planes headed their way. Collis realized that his phosphorescent wake stood out like a torch on a gloomy night just inviting attention, so he slowed to 20 knots. That helped a little but not enough, so he slowed to 15 knots. That was a lot better, and by midnight the small group was clear of the area. From all indications, the Japanese fleet was far to the east and the Japanese planes had returned to their base at Munda. Lt Cmdr Collis received a legion of merit and promotion to full Commander for his night's work. The ships received a Presidential Unit Citation as well as congratulations from COMSOPAC.

For at least one ship in the Japanese navy, the minefield laid that night was a shattering blow to her ego. Dodging PT Boat torpedoes, the 1900-ton Japanese destroyer MAKIGUMO tried sneaking down the coast of Guadalcanal as she had so many times in the past. For a time the Japanese crew thought their skipper had managed to pull another fast one. Then a shattering explosion broke the silence of the night. MAKIGUMO had found one of the mines laid by MINDIV ONE. There was no time for salvage, no time to tow her to safer waters, no time for much of anything except to open her sea cocks and let the sea claim the first Japanese vessel to fall victim to an American offensive minefield. For the Japanese it was more than offensive; it was downright embarrassing. Though this was the first, it would not be the last offensive minefield to claim a Japanese victim before control of the Solomon Islands was wrestled from them. There would be more.

The next shot at the Japanese was off the coast of Kolombangara Island. This island was blessed with an Australian coast watcher, the same one who had called for help when President Kennedy's PT was sunk. It was a well-fortified island in 1943 when the GAMBLE, BREESE, and PREBLE headed up that way on May the 4th. Their target was the narrow and forbidding Blackett Straits through which Japanese forces on

**1900-ton Japanese destroyer Makigumo, the first Japanese vessel to
fall victim to an American offensive mine field.**

Kolombangara were being supplied at night by Japanese barges and supply ships running down from the Shortland Islands.

Some nights, Japanese cruisers and destroyers ran along hoping to find fat targets. COMSOPAC decided enough was enough and that a little surprise party in the form of a string of mines was in order.

The BREESE, GAMBLE, and PREBLE loaded mines at Segund Channel in the Hebrides from the SS JAMES McPHERSON, and sailed on the 4th for Tulagi, a convenient stopping place where they could refuel from the SS ERSKINE PHELPS before continuing up The Slot. There too, they met up with the destroyer RADFORD, a new 2100 ton flush decker under the command of Commander W K Rosomer. RADFORD had radar, something lacking in the minelayers, and would act as guide through the narrow passages. Besides, she had a little more firepower with her twin mount 5" and her new 20mm and 44mm guns. She could stir up quite a response if opposition developed. She might not be able to hold off a division of cruisers, or even destroyers, but she was a lot better at it than any of the minelayers. The ships left late in the afternoon and headed northeast from Florida Harbor.

It wasn't the best of weather which was just as well. No moon, deep clouds, and multiple squalls hung over the area, now and again splashing down on the little formation as if the water had been poured out of a bucket. A signalman on the GAMBLE named Petrofsky said at one point when they were going through a squall, "I don't think that stuff has fallen far enough to break up into drops yet." He was at least partly right. It was a nasty night.

Between a leaky boiler on the GAMBLE and a defective fire room blower on the BREESE, the fleet was slowed to 25 knots. Generally they ran at 28. At 1910 hours, the RADFORD found a plane with her radar that could not be identified as friendly. After a bit of radio chatter it was determined that it was a navy Black Cat out searching for trouble, and was of no concern to the group of minelayers.

Code-named FIFTH AVENUE, the trip up through narrow Ferguson Passage was anything but a ride up Fifth Avenue. Old charts indicated the passage should be about 3500 yards wide between the reefs. The RADFORD found with her radar that the distance was considerably less, like maybe 2200 yards. About half way through the narrow channel, another blinding rain storm hit the formation. It was hard to tell if the ships were above or below water. Except that the water running across the decks was fresh, they might have been four submarines running partially submerged. But on they sped, each not knowing exactly where the other was except for the RADFORD which was blessed with radar.

The BREESE got nervous and broke radio silence to "Request a mark on commencement" as if she were going to a graduation. The RADFORD responded with a terse "Wilco. Wilco," and a minute later announced over the TBS, "Mark. I am turning. That is all." It was 0005 hours on May 7 when the mines started tumbling off the sterns of the minelayers. By 0023 hours, all mines had splashed over the stern and the RADFORD led the minelayers out through Blackett Straits, and turned west. They were home for breakfast the next morning at Florida Island. The PREBLE had some engine troubles and didn't join up with the GAMBLE and BREESE when they returned to Espiritu and Segund Channel.

After anchoring, a few sailors off the GAMBLE went over to the DIXIE, a repair ship which was a permanent resident of Segund Channel, to see what they could scrounge. While waiting at the head of the gangway for a return ride, a GAMBLE sailor overheard some sailor from the DIXIE talking to the Officer of the Deck. The CO asked the sailor why there were only two minelayers on the hook instead of three as there had been so many times in the past. The sailor said, "Why, didn't you hear? The PREBLE was sunk a couple days ago on a mine run into the upper Solomons." The GAMBLE sailors protests to the contrary did no good. As far as the DIXIE crew was concerned, when a ship failed to return from a mission it had obviously been sunk, and that was that.

The Japanese fleet found the newly planted minefield just as operations had figured they would. On May 4th, 1943, four Japanese destroyers started through Blackett Straits just like they had a license guaranteeing them free passage. They failed to complete the passage as planned. At 0700 that morning Sub-Lieutenant A R Evans, a coast watcher on Kolombangara, reported to Guadalcanal that there were three ships in the passage, one on fire, one crippled, and another trying to help. He didn't know that another had sunk before dawn. That one was the KUROSHIO.

That was what the aircraft on Henderson Field had been waiting for. "Saddle up boys! We have a stationary target" rolled across the flight line. Within two hours more than sixty SBDs, TBFs, F4Us, and P40s were over the target area bombing and strafing. Someone nailed OYASHIO, the only one undamaged, with a thousand pound bomb and the last of the four proud vessels finally felt the sting of war. MICHISIO, though "burning merrily" according to the coast watcher, did make it out of those waters and survived to fight another day. The others were either sunk or stranded. The minefield, so carefully laid, claimed at least three of Japan's fighting ships within 24 hours after completing their mission. Most of the minefield still remained to capture other ships if they dared to enter those waters.

May was a busy month for this group of minelayers. There was little rest for the crews and a great deal of danger. After returning to Segund Channel, they once again took on a full load of mines from the same SS JAMES McPHERSON and on May 12th, they were again on their way to The Slot. The RADFORD must have liked their company for she was once again steaming in the van. They were quite a team.

This time their target was Kula Gulf between Kolombangara and New Georgia Islands. They sneaked in close to shore and laid 255 mines just off the reef. This time they were not alone. Cruisers and destroyers were there in force, and while the minelayers laid their deadly cargo in the water, the cruisers and destroyers laid a bit further off shore and shelled the airfield at Munda and the port facilities at Vella. From the decks of the minelayers, it was a colorful rainbow of glowing dots slowly passing overhead.

Sailing directly under the arc of fire, it was at once both a frightening and a glorious experience. Some of the crew would have probably rather been somewhere else, and some would find themselves in similar situations in later invasions during the war. As one gunner on the BREESE said, "What if one of those gun captains forgets to put one bag of powder in one of those eight inch shells? It might fall a little short." But none did.

As praise for this mission, Admiral Halsey sent his own personal congratulations and a commendation to the commanding officers of all ships that participated. The citation read, in part: "For skillful and effective performance of duty in the line of his profession as Commanding Officer of a fast minelayer on mining missions into enemy waters, through restricted waters in total darkness, laying an effective mine field, undetected by the enemy, to within a thousand yards of an enemy-held coast line." Captain Armstrong, skipper of the GAMBLE, had copies made and distributed to each crew member with a note crediting the crew with making the citation possible.

After Kula Gulf, the minelayers had a few days off. The GAMBLE spent her time running down to Sydney for ten days of R and R plus a few necessary repairs. The skipper talked to the crew the day before arrival and stated they would have an almost open gangway for their stay—except that everyone would have to report for morning muster at 0800 hours every day. Muster would be brief and the men were encouraged to "cut loose and enjoy." For the old GAMBLE, moving into colder waters off Australia proved to create some unforeseen problems. There had been no hot water in the crew showers for months but with Australia being in the middle of winter, the near freezing waters coming out of the shower heads proved too much for even the tough old sailors of the GAMBLE. Someone in the engine room finally remembered how to get steam to the water heating jackets in the shower rooms and the crew enjoyed their first hot showers in over ten months.

The ten days went by much more quickly than the crew would have liked. Hardly anyone was happy to be heading back up north but duty called, and away they went back to the Solomons. They stopped briefly at Noumea to meet up with BREESE and PREBLE and to pick up a load of mines at Duco Penninsula. They refueled at Efate in the Hebrides and then steamed up to Tulagi where they awaited departure for more adventures dropping their 500 pound eggs into enemy waters. They left Florida Harbor on June 29, 1943 with a new escort, the PRINGLE. The trip up The Slot was uneventful and the weather was, as usual, lousy: heavy squalls, lightning, and a sheer wind that threatened to swing them off course.

It was actually one of the more pleasant trips if you call steaming into enemy waters and laying mines a pleasant experience. The mines went into the water right on schedule and right on target, and the retreat back to Florida Harbor was uneventful. The Japanese were a long time discovering this field. It lay quietly in the water and found no prey until November 25, 1944 when the Japanese submarine RO-100 tried to sneak her way past the Shortland and found a mine. She discovered it was still very active. Check off one more submarine for the American minelayers and a watery grave for a Japanese submarine crew. No surface vessels ever found the field. The RO-100 was its only victim.

The same night, the DMS ZANE was unloading troops of the 169th Infantry Regiment east of Rendova Island and suddenly found herself aground on an uncharted reef. There were plenty of those in the area and her finding one in the dead of the night came as no surprise to either her skipper or to COMSOPAC which immediately sent the RAIL, a former mine layer and sweeper turned tug, up to tow her clear.

Vella Lavella had already been the scene of two battles between American and Japanese forces: the Battle of Kolombangara on July 13 and the Battle of Vella Lavella on August 6th and 7th. The destroyer GWIN had been sunk in the first, together with damage to two cruisers and another destroyer. The Japanese didn't get away scott free. We managed to sink the Japanese cruiser JINTSU. In the second battle we fared much better, sinking the Japanese destroyer KAWAKAZE with no losses of our own. With all the action in the area, our leaders decided it would be easier to try another method.

The idea of going gun for gun with the Japanese was a little bit distasteful if a simpler method could be arranged, so another mine-laying expedition was decreed.

The night of August 24, 1943 found three of the old four stack minelayers, BREESE, PREBLE, and MONTGOMERY steaming along through the slot heading for Vella Lavella with destroyer PRINGLE along for guidance and support. Also along, for "just in case" were American destroyers NICHOLAS, O'BANNON, TAYLOR, and CHEVALIER. They thought it might be fun to drop a few shells on the Japanese airfield at Munda as well.

This trip was not to be uneventful as some of the others had been. Just a scant 90 miles from their target lay the Japanese airfield at Kahili, fully manned and prepared to repel boarders. Their pilots didn't think too much of American ships playing around in their front yard and were going to let any American forces who came their way know it.

To make matters worse, a seaman on PREBLE, S 1/c T R Flud, decided just after darkness closed over the ships that he had appendicitis. The Chief Pharmacist Mate, Cantmill, agreed. The kid probably wouldn't last till daylight unless something was done in a hurry. So Cantmill laid the lad out on the wardroom table and with the help of Lt G W Winkleman, carved out the inflamed appendix. No more complications were discovered and Flud recovered with little more than a faint scar to show for his experience.

Meanwhile the ships sped on. At 0100 on the 25th, they started their mine planting. Enemy snoopers (the planes from Kahili) were overhead to get a good look at what was going on. A total of 183 mines went into the water just as nice as you please and by 0056, MONTGOMERY dropped her last mine and started to make a turn to starboard to get into position to make good her retreat. Either the MONTGOMERY started too soon or the PREBLE started too late because before corrective action could be taken by MONTGOMERY, she found the PREBLE slicing along her starboard side. The MONTGOMERY backed emergency full but the damage had been done. Both ships were damaged, the MONTGOMERY much more seriously. Luckily no sailors on either ship were injured.

The MONTGOMERY found herself able to do only ten knots and enemy planes still circled overhead. Survival didn't seem to be in the cards but there was little point in laying-to and letting the Japanese have a shot at them. So the ships sped on as best they could. At 0137, a flare lit the area and everyone topside thought surely they would come under attack. Nothing happened. A few minutes later a MONTGOMERY lookout spotted a plane and again everyone held his breath. But the plane apparently didn't see them, and they were once again able to breathe a sigh of relief.

They sped on. At 0313 hours, another flare blazed just astern of the MONTGOMERY. She seemed to be getting all the attention and didn't appreciate it one bit. Almost immediately after the flare burst into flame, two bombs hit the water about 200 yards off her port beam. The only casualty from this near miss was Stewards Mate M P Gozalo who received just enough of a scratch to earn a purple heart. Twenty minutes later two more bombs hit the water but were far enough astern of the MONTGOMERY that they did no damage. The MONTGOMERY ducked into a rain squall and escaped with nothing more than a few shrapnel scratches. The crew heaved a vast sigh of relief. At daybreak,

Together with the derivative P-63 Kingcobra, the P-39 Airacobra was one of the most successful fixed-wing aircraft manufactured by Bell, and welcome cover for the minelayers.

nine P-39 fighters showed up to provide cover, and it appeared the long ordeal was over. Later in the day the tug PAWNEE showed her mast over the horizon and was soon alongside the MONTGOMERY to take her in tow. PREBLE and BREESE stayed along to provide screening, and before the day was over, they were all back in Purvis Bay at Florida Island across from Guadalcanal.

The next safari into enemy waters was even further north. The Island of Bougainville was scheduled for a landing of United States Marines in the early hours of November 1, 1943, another step in the march to Japan. Leading the transports hauling the marines into the beach were the destroyer minesweepers HOVEY and HOPKINS sweeping for moored mines. Right behind were two more DMs, the DORSEY and SOUTHARD sweeping for magnetic mines with their cute little electric tails dragging behind. The HOVEY and HOPKINS lost all their paravanes on uncharted coral reefs and pinnacles but stayed around to lend whatever assistance they could. All four were still there when a group of Japanese dive bombers and fighter planes came to pay a visit—welcoming committee, so to speak. They stayed twenty-five minutes during the lunch hour and managed to damage the cruiser BIRMINGHAM and the transports FULLER and PRESIDENT JACKSON. One dive bomber narrowly missed the HOVEY by less than 50 yards. The HOVEY missed him too even though she fired twelve 3" shells and 65 rounds of 20mm ammo in less than 10 seconds.

The Destroyer *USS Renshaw* reported to the Pacific Fleet in the spring of 1943, and protected minelayers and transports in the Solomon Islands area.

Of course this wasn't the only action going on in the area. Just after midnight on 2 November, the TRACY and PRUITT, led by the EATON, planted a field of 176 mines near Otua Island. They returned again on the 8th and laid another field in the same area. This field had been set for delayed action but still a number of premature explosions were heard as the minefield was laid. No records came to light of Japanese vessels being sunk by these fields but it is almost certain they had their effect in keeping Japanese shipping from the area.

But the real action the night of November 2 was to be had by a squadron of cruisers and destroyers that were cruising just off the south coast of Bougainville waiting for Japanese reinforcements. The Japanese were aware of their presence but just didn't know exactly where they were, even though they were looking for them. It took another mine-laying group, the GAMBLE, BREESE, and SICARD to get the snoopers to drop a flare and disclose the fact they were in the area. Escorted by the RENSHAW, the three minelayers were there to lay a field off Cape Moltke, just 15 miles west of Torokina Beach where the Marines had landed the day before. This was planned to stop any attempted force that might try to sweep around Cape Moltke and raise hell among the transports.

At 0100 hours on November 2nd, the mine-laying group was in position to start mine-laying operations. A float plane bantered around overhead but so far had dropped no flares. The nervous gunners were under strict orders not to fire and give the ships position

Coming from Pearl Harbor, Destroyer Mine Layer *USS Sicard* joined her sister ships *Gamble* and *Breeze* in Purvis Bay forming a fast minelaying group.

away. That was sound advice. The ships were well within range of Japanese coastal guns manned by equally nervous Japanese gunners, who needed little more than an indication where the ships were to start firing. At 0110 hours, with Cape Moltke bearing 340 at 4,500 yards, the mines started splashing into the water right on schedule. By this time all the layers had their own radar and all the navigators were well-experienced, so they should have known exactly where they were. Perhaps they did since they all agreed where the mines were placed in a post-operation conference. But when the mines were swept on October 12, 1944, they were found to be a good ten miles from where the charts indicated they should be.

The mines were all planted in the usual fifteen minute interval allotted to such activities. Flares fell from snoopers a couple of times during the run, but they were some distance away and no one was sure they had been spotted, even though the snoopers stayed in the same area for a long time. As soon as the mines were properly placed, the minelayers and their escort headed out of the area. They immediately met two divisions of American destroyers and a cruiser division heading in the other direction. They passed close aboard at 0230 hours.

USS Braine, **destroyer escort for the minelayers** *Gamble* **and** *Breese* **as they planted the largest single minefield in the Solomons.**

The Battle of Empress Augusta Bay began at 0247. The minelayers had accomplished a successful mine-planting and escaped by the skin of their teeth. Securing from general quarters a few minutes after passing the cruisers and destroyers, the mine group was unaware of the existence of a massive Japanese fleet being so close. A sonar man on the GAMBLE stepped out of the sound shack on the bridge and glanced casually to starboard and thought he noted heat lightning. The lightning quickly took the form of several red dots slowly rising into the night sky and getting bigger each moment. He realized that what he had seen was the flack from some very big guns and the red dots were shells headed in his direction. The OD spotted them about the same time and rang the general alarm before most of the crew had a chance to get more than a few feet from their stations. They remained at general quarters for another hour before they felt safe enough to escape the battle.

A few days later, the TRACY, BREESE, GAMBLE, and SICARD were back with the BRAINE leading the way. On November 8th, they planted 385 mines near Otua Island to keep the Japanese from sneaking down the northeast side of the island. This was the largest single field planted in the Solomons.

Just a couple of weeks later the same group was back again. At 0002 hours on November 24th, they started laying mines just a few miles from Moila Point at Bougainville in Turube Channel. They laid 340 mines in the water, thus closing all access to the Shortland Island area. This was tough on the GAMBLE sailors who were involved with getting the mines off the tracks and into the water, because the launching gear jammed just before the last fourteen mines went into the water. The last fourteen went into the water by sheer, brute strength, but into the water they went, nevertheless. As if that wasn't enough of a problem, the steering cable then went on the blink and steering was lost for a few minutes. The GAMBLE's resolute sailors soon had this repaired, though, and they were able to maneuver clear of the area with the rest of the ships.

In the narrow passage between Buka Island and the extreme northwest tip of Bougainville, a natural passage existed which was just perfect for the use of Japanese supply barges. There they could pass almost totally unobserved by American forces. It had been mined by air on November 16, 1943 when Navy, Marine, and Royal New Zealand planes planted 42 mines that they had picked up at Mine Assembly Depot #4 on Guadalcanal. This did little good to stem the tide of supplies that were pouring through the narrow passage; so on May 2, 1944, the SICARD and BREESE with the destroyer HALFORD along for company, dropped 170 mines near Taiof Island. They returned to Espiritu for another load and again on May 8 with the HALFORD, the FULLAM, and the HUDSON, they laid another 170 mines in East Buka Passage. Still the Japanese supply barges were getting through. Somehow they had to put a stop to this nonsense. The Japanese vessels were ducking in and out of estuaries and bays too shallow for the old DMs to get into, so another tactic had to be devised.

In mid-May, a group of PT Boats were sent up from the Treasury Islands. They scouted along the coast, checked the charts they had against actual soundings, and decided the only way to totally blockade the area was to do some shallow water mining. They chose LCI landing craft for the job. On May 18th, the LCI 18 and LCI 58, carrying mines supplied and outfitted at Torokina by Mine Detail #15, snuck into the mouths of the Hongoria, Mobiai, Mibo, and Puriata Rivers and left three mines in each. That ended mine-laying in the Solomon Islands.

Japanese sweep forces in the area were almost nonexistent. After the war, Commander Yunoki of the Japanese Navy, said the Japanese were well-aware of all the plants that were made in the upper Solomons, but there was little they could do to sweep them and clear a path for their own ships. He noted that all of these fields made re-supply of the Japanese forces very difficult and that even he himself had a most difficult time escaping through the mine fields. He found it necessary to get away in a small wooden boat. As time passed a few Japanese sweepers did show up but the fields still claimed 3

Japanese destroyers. Two or three Japanese submarines that disappeared in the area were probably the victims of our mine fields.

The overall count of mines laid in the Solomons was very impressive considering the means of delivery. In all, the DMs planted 13 fields in 34 sorties. Many of the old DMs made over six runs each. In total, they planted 2,617 mines. All were Mark VI types, some with modifications, refurbished from stocks remaining from the North Sea Mine Barrage. In addition, the LCIs planted another 12 in the river entrances of Southwest Bougainville. Those planted by the LCIs were magnetic mines designated Mark 13-5.

When the war started, there were eight old four stackers that had been converted to destroyer mine layers. They were the GAMBLE (DM-15), the RAMSAY (DM-16), the MONTGOMERY (DM-17), the BREESE (DM-18), the TRACY (DM-19), the PREBLE (DM-20), the SICARD (DM-21), and the PRUITT (DM-22). All of them but the GAMBLE and MONTGOMERY survived the war. Only the RAMSAY didn't take part in the mine-laying runs in the Solomon Islands. The BREESE made more runs than any of the others, having dared the waters of the upper Solomons seven times. The GAMBLE and TRACY made six runs each sharing the honor of second place.

Let's take a look at what became of these venerable old cans. On February 17th, 1945, two 250-pound bombs hit the GAMBLE and badly damaged it while on patrol off Iwo Jima. Five men lost their lives, one was missing, and eight were wounded. The next day, as the marines were pouring ashore at Iwo, the DORSEY took her in tow and got her out of range of more damage. She was then turned over to the LSM-126 and towed back to Agana Harbor at Guam. There she was declared unfit for future duty, taken to sea and sunk by our own gun fire. The GAMBLE earned seven battle stars for service in the South Pacific.

The RAMSAY was the only DM that didn't get a chance to participate in the night mine runs into the upper Solomons. She did her share of other mine-laying, having laid many defensive fields at Espiritu, Efate, the Fiji Islands, Samoa, and other locations. The RAMSAY earned three battle stars for service in the South Pacific. She was decommissioned 19 October, 1945, struck from the navy list 13 November, 1945, and sold for scrap on 22 June, 1946.

MONTGOMERY drifted into a mine while at anchor at the east end of Angulu Island, Palau, in the Caroline Group on 17 October, 1944. The explosion killed four men. On 21

October, she was towed to Ulithi where temporary repairs were made by the VESTAL. It was not until 12 January, 1945 that she was able to get under way under her own power when she sailed for Pearl Harbor and then San Francisco, arriving there on 13 February, 1945. A survey recommended she be decommissioned, and at 1400 hours on April 23, 1945, the commission pennant was hauled down the final time. The MONTGOMERY earned four battle stars for service it WWII. She was sold for scrap on 11 March, 1946.

The BREESE, the most experienced of the minelayers with seven runs into the upper Solomons, earned ten battle stars for service during WWII. She was decommissioned 15 January, 1946, and sold for scrap 16 May, 1946.

The TRACY was the first ship into Nagasaki Wan (tide station) in Japanese home waters after the war ended. She stayed several months before returning to the United States where she was decommissioned on 21 November, 1945 and sold for scrap in 1946. TRACY earned seven battle stars for service in WWII.

The PREBLE was re-designated as a miscellaneous auxiliary vessel (AG-99) on 5 June, 1945. She was decommissioned on 7 December, 1945 and sold for scrap. The PREBLE earned eight battle stars in WWII.

The SICARD was reclassified AG-100 on 5 June 1945, Decommissioned 21 November, 1945 and sold for scrap 22 June, 1946. The SICARD earned two battle stars for service in WWII.

The PRUITT was re-designated AG-101 on 5 June, 1945 and ordered to be deactivated on 21 September, 1945. She was decommissioned at Philadelphia, struck from the navy list on 5 December, 1945 and sold for scrap. The PRUITT earned three battle stars for service in WWII.

Collectively, as a select group, the old DMs probably earned more citations than any other group of equal size. Living conditions were never the best, food was not of the quality or the quantity that was found on the larger ships of the fleet, but the crews seldom complained, and they were proud of their ships and their shipmates. They worked well together as a team and supported each other ashore and afloat. The memories shared by the crew members will never fade from our minds. The ships and men all served In the proudest traditions of naval service. As some wag once said, "She's not much on liberty, but she's a home and a feeder." ⚓

Gamble Kills Japanese Sub I - 123

Excerpted from the book *Tin Cans* by Theodore Roscoe

Operating with the Jap fleet in the Solomons arena was an Advance Expeditionary Force of submarines. The force contained eight submarines, all but one with "I" numbers. The odd one was RO-34. In August the submarines began to rear their ugly periscope heads in the waters east of Guadalcanal.

It remained for an old "four piper," an ex-DD, to wipe out the first of the subs that went down in the enemy's Guadalcanal offensive. The old timer was the USS GAMBLE. Converted into a destroyer-minelayer, GAMBLE was on duty off Guadalcanal as an A/S vessel. At 0805 in the morning of August 29, her lookouts sighted the conning tower of a large submarine some 9,000 yards distant.

GAMBLE's skipper, Lieutenant Commander S. N. Tackney, snapped the crew into action. Though the old four piper had taken up mine laying as a vocation, she still carried depth charge gear. She attacked the sub with "ash cans" at 0844, and kept at it for the next three hours.

After her last attack, made at 1147, a large quantity of oil surged to the surface, bearing in its dark tide the splintered remnants of deck planking. The kill was eventually verified by Japanese records opened for post-war inspection. In the blood-stained waters off Guadalcanal, GAMBLE had sunk I-123.

As a footnote to history, GAMBLE's number before conversion to a DM was also 123. In an even odder coincidence, the 1-123 was originally designed as a mine-laying submarine so both vessels were in the same line of work. The 1-123 was also the submarine that went to French Frigate Shoals and supplied the Emily flying boats with gas in March, 1942 for the second attack on Pearl Harbor.

The first Japanese submarine casualty of the WWII Solomons Campaign was the special mine laying submarine I-123, sunk off the coast of Malaita on August 29, 1942, by the the *USS Gamble* (DM-15). The photo depicts a sister sub, the I-122.

The Japanese Prisoner Aboard the USS Ballard

A Personal Account by Dick Russell WT 1/c USS Gamble

During our Baton Rouge reunion, Mike Tackney passed out copies of three letters that were written to him from a Japanese prisoner we had transported from Midway to Pearl Harbor. Several of the fellows that received the copies had no idea what the story was concerning that incident. I was there and would like to pass on the story as I saw it, augmented by some research I did later.

During the Midway battle, the Imperial Japanese Navy aircraft carrier *Hiryu* (*Flying Dragon*) was hit by four bombs delivered by our dive bombers. The four direct hits set off fires and explosions and soon turned *Hiryu* into a blazing hulk. Fire spread among the loaded planes on deck and cut off all passageways to the engine rooms. Two desperate attempts to gain access to the engine rooms were unsuccessful. Finally, it became clear that there was no hope of saving the ship. *Hiryu's* crew was ordered to abandon ship at 0230 hours, June 5, 1942 and her escort destroyers were ordered to pump torpedoes into the burning wreck. One of those torpedo explosions opened a passageway that allowed thirty-eight men trapped in the engine rooms to escape to a whale boat, and *Hiryu* shortly thereafter went to the bottom.

The thirty-eight engineers were adrift (one book says for two weeks) until they were picked up and made prisoners by the USS BALLARD. By the time BALLARD found them, four of the sailors had died and thirty-three others were in very poor condition. BALLARD turned her prisoners over to the marines on Midway.

My ship, the destroyer-minelayer USS GAMBLE DM-15, sailed from Pearl Harbor on June 11, 1942, escorting the first supply ships to reach Midway after the battle. We arrived at Midway on June 17. The passage was uneventful. At this point, I became involved as a participant-observer of the prisoner affair and record my own experience.

Japanese Aircraft Carrier *Hiryu* at Anchor in Yokosuka Shortly after Completion in 1939.

***Hiryu* Running Speed Trials on 28 April, 1939.**

I was curious about the battle damage on Midway and managed to get ashore on the morning of June 23. The ubiquitous gooney birds seemed unperturbed by the recent events and had to be stepped around or over while I toured part of the island. I collected as a souvenir a Japanese bomb fragment from the wall of one of the many bomb craters. When I returned to the ship, there was some unusual activity going on: mess stewards were removing the Captain's gear from his cabin, located on the main deck just below the bridge, and were taking it below. The ship fitters had closed the battle ports in the Captain's cabin and had tightened the dogs with pipe wrenches, then sawed the wings off the wing nuts. I soon learned that a brig was being jury-rigged and that we were to ship a Japanese prisoner. The prisoner was Commander Kunizo Aiso, the chief engineering officer in the carrier *Hiryu*, one of the thirty-four survivors picked up by the BALLARD.

Battle of Midway, June 1942. Left: Japanese Aircraft Carrier _Hiryu_ maneuvers to avoid three sticks of bombs dropped during a high-level attack by B-17 bombers, shortly after 8 am, 4 June 1942. Right: _Hiryu_ shortly before being scuttled after the Battle of Midway.

Nothing could have kept me from getting a good look at the enemy at close range, so when the whale boat came along side with the prisoner, I was only a few paces away from the boarding ladder and took in the scene with great interest. During that watch, Lt. (j.g.) R. E. Carpenter was the OD and responsible for conducting the formalities. A marine guard came up the ladder first followed by Aiso and a second marine was behind him. Aiso was wearing U. S. Navy blue dungarees, black Navy shoes, and no cap. He had two small identical silver insignias, one in each wing of his open shirt collar. He was carrying a small blue canvas travel bag. He was about five feet four inches, slender build. His face was very brown, but he showed no other effects from his days adrift. It was hard to guess his age but seemed to be in his forties. He wasn't at all cowed in attitude— seemed to take everything in as he stepped on deck. I caught his eye for a split second—it made me feel uneasy. It is a rare event today when a sailor can see his enemy eye-to-eye.

The boarding party lined up abreast with the diminutive Aiso flanked by his marine guards facing Carpenter. Carpenter saluted the commander. No one returned his salute. The two marine guards stood stony-faced looking straight ahead and Aiso gave Carpenter an abbreviated bow. Carpenter asked the party to follow and they crossed the well deck and went into the Captain's cabin. Within a few minutes, after Carpenter signed for the

52

Survivors of *Hiryu* aboard *USS Ballard*, June 1942.

Survivors of *Hiryu* being transferred from the *USS Ballard* to Midway, June 1942.

Japanese prisoners of war, survivors of the Japanese aircraft carrier *Hiryu*, are brought ashore at Midway following their rescue from an open lifeboat by *USS Ballard* (AVD-10), 19 June 1942. After being held for a few days on Midway, they were sent on to Pearl Harbor on 23 June. Note US Marine guards armed with M1903 Springfield rifles.

prisoner, the marine guards departed leaving Aiso in the jury-rigged brig. A chief petty officer armed with a .45 automatic stood guard at the door.

A few hours later on June 23, we cleared the reef off Midway Island bound for Pearl Harbor. It wasn't until later in the afternoon that I had an opportunity to talk with the chief who had the first watch guarding the prisoner. One of Aiso's marine guards told the CPO that he had hoped that Aiso would do something while being transferred to justify shooting him. The marine had a deep and abiding hate for the "little bastard" and told the CPO to kill Aiso if given the slightest provocation. To feel a dislike for the enemy is a natural enough reaction, but this absolute loathing for Aiso rose to another, higher order of magnitude.

Cutter from the sunken Imperial Japanese aircraft carrier *Hiryu*, suspended from the starboard boat davits of *USS Ballard* (AVD-10), at Midway in late June 1942. The cutter had been picked up on 19 June, along with its occupants, who became prisoners of war. Note the 77-foot ELCO-type PT boat (either the *USS PT-25* or *PT-30*) visible in the left background. Also note *Ballard's* motor whale boat, cane fender, dark-colored awnings and smokestack details.

There were thirty-eight sailors who took to the lifeboat, four died while adrift and thirty-three were in poor condition when the BALLARD found them. But not so Commander Aiso. He had commandeered all of the food and water for his personal use. This act of callous disregard and evil cruelty was to us unthinkable. The epithet "little bastard" had taken on a more substantial meaning. By suppertime on the first day out, we had more reason to dislike Aiso. When the mess steward brought his supper, the Commander gave it a cursory glance and threw a temper tantrum. "Everything was soaked in grease"—he wanted plain boiled white rice and some fish or beef not cooked in grease. He also ordered some novels to read. He ordered the steward out and the food with him. There was no language barrier: Aiso had attended an American university.

USS Ballard **(AVD-1), the ship that rescued the survivors of the *Hiryu*, underway, 21 March 1941, location unknown.**

Our Captain was Lieutenant Commander S. N. Tackney. When he received the news of the Commander's behavior, he had the bridge talker contact the wardroom and ordered the communications officer to report to the bridge immediately. When the officer arrived, the Captain told him to relay to Aiso that he would eat the food that was served him or not eat at all!

On the second day out, Aiso registered another complaint, the exact nature of it, I never learned. But when it was reported to Captain Tackney, he had the communications officer relate to Aiso that "no further complaints from Commander Nuisance would be tolerated." Aiso evidently saw the light, so he clammed up and sulked in his bunk and refused to take his half-hour exercise periods on the well deck. We soon reached Pearl Harbor, and as we nosed in toward the fuel dock, a marine detachment was waiting to take off the prisoner. A marine sergeant and three privates came aboard as soon as the brow was lowered. Our CPO guard brought Aiso out. They were standing on the well deck and Aiso's small blue canvas bag was on the deck near his feet. When the detachment was ready to leave, Aiso wanted one of the marines to carry his bag. The marine sergeant quickly kicked Aiso in the behind and told him to pick up the bag and move out.

That was the last I saw of this little brown man. Four husky marines marched Aiso briskly down the quay, as he carried his little blue bag. ⚓

Some Important Dates in the Life of the
USS Gamble (DM-15)

In early December I received a call from Lieutenant Peterson, the last Commanding Officer of the USS GAMBLE. He stated he had numerous pages of the GAMBLE log as well as many pictures of crewmen, special events that had occurred on the GAMBLE, and a reel of micro-film which covered the GAMBLE during most of 1943. Unfortunately I found the micro-film of the 1943 log mostly unreadable with the equipment I had available so I can't specify the dates and times of many of our mine runs into the upper Solomons. Most of those runs are detailed in "Offensive Mine Laying by Surface Craft during the Second World War, Pacific Theater" beginning on page 17, and those dates and times were obtained from my historical research files which I have accumulated over the past eight years.

There is some disagreement between Commander Lott's book, *Most Dangerous Sea*, and the records I have unearthed. This is often the case in doing historical research. I have found that eyewitness accounts of events most often do not agree with the historical record. I'm not sure if this is because each participant has a unique and individual perspective, or is the result of faulty memory. Even as to the number of deaths on a given ship, I find disagreement. For instance, in the case of the sinking of the USS SALUTE at Borneo, Friday, 8 June, 1945, I find four different reports on dead and wounded. ALL HANDS says 9 dead, 8 wounded. Karig says 9 dead, 37 wounded. Elliot says 6 dead, 37 wounded. Another says 5 dead, 12 wounded. I have not examined the ship's log which may be the only way I will ever determine an accurate number. In spite of all the research I have done and the number of GAMBLE survivors I have talked to, I was not aware of Ensign PRITCHARD's death until I reviewed the GAMBLE logs.

The following dates are somewhat from the log sheets sent by Lieutenant Peterson, and somewhat from my recollections, and somewhat from my research, and somewhat from information sent to me by various former crewmen of the GAMBLE, or, in some cases, by direct interviews with former crew members. I hope the dates are accurate and none of you finds too much fault with them. If you DO find me to be in error, I would appreciate very much if you would let me know so I can make corrections in my files.

"Red Lead Row", San Diego Destroyer Base, California. at the end of 1922, with at least 65 destroyers tied up there. U.S. Naval Historical Center Photograph.

19 November, 1918: The USS GAMBLE (DD-123) was placed in commission at Norfolk Navy Base, Norfolk, Virginia.

17 June, 1922: GAMBLE was decommissioned at Destroyer Base, San Diego, California and placed in "Red Lead Row."

24 May, 1930: GAMBLE was re-commissioned at Destroyer Base, San Diego, California.

13 June, 1930: GAMBLE was reclassified as Light Minelayer DM-15.

22 December, 1937: GAMBLE was decommissioned at Destroyer Base, San Diego, California.

25 September, 1939: The USS GAMBLE (DM-15) was re-commissioned at San Diego, California.

31 September, 1939: The number on the bow of GAMBLE was changed from 123 to 15, even though she had been designated as DM-15 since 13 June, 1930.

20 October, 1939: GAMBLE sailed to Vallejo, California for repairs and alterations.

December, 1939: GAMBLE collided with the USS MONTGOMERY while attempting to anchor in San Pablo Bay after rehabilitation work at the Naval Shipyard in Vallejo.

7 December, 1941: Moored in nest with RAMSAY and MONTGOMERY in Middle Loch, Pearl Harbor off Pearl City, Territory of Hawaii, when Japanese planes began their attack on Pearl Harbor at 0755. She sortied around 1000 for off-shore patrol, picking up the Commanding Officer and the Executive Officer en route to the entrance. Later in the day she fired on a friendly submarine which was attempting to surface just outside the entrance to the harbor.

Mark VI Sea Mine with Schematic.

June, 1942: GAMBLE escorted a resupply convoy to Midway Island just after the battle of Midway. She returned escorting a large number of PT Boats which had participated in that battle.

Wednesday, 22 July, 1942: GAMBLE left West Lock in company with TRACY and BREESE loaded with 84 Mark VI contact mines.

Saturday, 25 July, 1942: 0918 Entered Palmyra Channel for fuel. 1008 Air raid alarm. John Sturak, AS, transferred to NAS Palmyra for treatment. 1600 Left Palmyra.

Sunday, 26 July, 1942: 1507 Sound gear went out. 1835 Crossed the equator. 2020 Sound gear repaired.

Friday, 31 July, 1942: Crossed the date line this date - dropped 30 July - 0154 Ship believed to be an oil tanker passed abeam 1600 yards; recognition signal given by GAMBLE but tanker responded incorrectly. (GAMBLE crew members may remember this as the night we had General Quarters without sounding the general alarm. Everyone was awakened by being shaken awake and told to report to battle stations). 0835 Entered Suva, Fiji Islands, channel. Left same day.

Sunday, 2 August, 1942: 0355 Sighted active volcano (Mount Benbow) on Ambrym Island, New Hebrides. 0936-1128 Practice mining runs. 1500-1609 Practice mining runs. 1716 Sighted ships in Palikula Bay.

The US Navy destroyer *USS Tucker* (DD-374) sunk at Bruat channel between Aore and Malo Island, south of Espiritu Santo, on 5 August 1942, after accidentally hitting a mine laid by the *Gamble* only the day before.

Monday, 3 August, 1942: 0930 Commenced mining - Laid 21 mines. 1300 Commenced mining run, 15 mines. 1353 Ran through Segond Channel. 1514 Started mine run, laid 21 mines and two marker buoy mines. 1659 Anchored in Segond Channel.

Tuesday, 4 August, 1942: 0804 Underway. 1300 Sighted USS CURTISS escorted by USS McFARLAND. 1350 Escorted USS CURTISS into Segond Channel. 1825 - Lt Cmdr Cox, USN, came aboard from NIRA LUCKENBACH. 0844 - USS TUCKER (DD 374) escorting the NIRA LUCKENBACH attempted to enter the west entrance to Segond Channel and exploded two mines planted the day before. Six men were killed by the explosion. Three bodies were recovered and buried at a newly established military cemetery on Espiritu Santos. The DICTIONARY OF AMERICAN FIGHTING SHIPS identifies the escorted vessel as NIRA LUCKENBACH, Lott says NORA. I have written to Armed Guard personnel who were on the NIRA LUCKENBACH and confirmed it was the NIRA. The GAMBLE log identifies her as NORA. There is no mention in the GAMBLE log of the TUCKER being sunk. Lott says six men killed - DAFS says three killed - also says she struck mine at 2145 and drifted all night before sinking the next day as YP 346 attempted to pull her to a nearby reef. I believe that Lott is correct in his time. I have corresponded with a man who was on board YP 346 that day and he confirms it was early in the day. I also know several former crew members of the TUCKER and they too confirm it happened early in the 0800-1200 watch. Such are the conflicts one runs into in doing historical research.

Gamble **crew members rescued four stranded aviators from the *USS Saratoga* on Nora Island on 29 August, 1942. *Saratoga,* above, at Pearl Harbor, June 6, 1942.**

Tuesday, 11 August, 1942: I believe this was the day a small working party went ashore on Aore Island to collect fruit and coconuts. We found a large quantity of bananas, oranges, coconuts, tangerines, mangoes, and papayas. Just as we were leaving, the plantation owner, on whose land we were scrounging for food, gave us a pig weighing about 200 pounds as well as about six dozen eggs, more or less fresh. By the time we left we discovered the GAMBLE had been sent out to off shore patrol so we had to go outside the channel to meet her. The whale boat was so heavily loaded we had but a few inches of freeboard but we managed to catch up with GAMBLE and everyone returned safely complete with eggs, pig, and fruit. I believe Toth butchered the pig, and we had a grand feast, not the least of which were the (more or less) fresh eggs.

Saturday, 29 August, 1942: 0805 Sighted enemy submarine on surface bearing 010 true, distance 5 miles. Went to General Quarters. 0810 shifted to main engines. 0815 Submarine submerged. For the next four hours we chased the submarine at various courses and speeds dropping, in total, 21 depth charges. 1006 U. S. Navy dive bomber relayed message to ship there was an Air Raid Alert in effect. 1215 Sighted debris in water believed to be deck planking from submarine. 1259 observed oil bubble. Submarine believed to have been sunk. 1330 Received message from U. S. Navy plane telling of four stranded aviators on island bearing 150T distance 10 miles. 1402 Boat left ship with Lt. (jg) J. H. Rayburn in charge to rescue aviators from Nura Island. (So much for my excellent memory - I would have sworn, and said so elsewhere in this book, that the boat left before we sighted the submarine). 1425 Boat returned and was hoisted aboard with one officer and three enlisted aviators from USS SARATOGA.

Sunday, 30 August, 1942: 1150 Received 5 Mark III and 10 Mark IV depth charges from USS LITTLE. (LITTLE and GREGORY, both old four stackers converted to APDs, were sunk by Japanese destroyers six days later off Savo Island). 1515 Went to General Quarters for Air Raid alert. 1525 Sighted flight of 18 enemy bombers bearing 240T, distant 10 miles. 1949 Sighted unidentified planes overhead. Went to Battle Stations.

Monday, 31 August, 1942: At General Quarters. 0030 Secured from General Quarters. 0135 Observed flashes and heard detonation of gunfire bearing 145T. 0400 Commenced receiving detachment of Marines aboard for transportation to Guadalcanal Island; 150 enlisted and 8 officers on board at 0500. 0537 Underway to escort US KOPARA to Guadalcanal. 0906 Commenced unloading Marines via landing boats from ships present. 0940 B. V. Gentle returned aboard from duties assigned in USS KOPARA. 1020 Went to General Quarters during air raid alert. Maneuvering at various courses and speeds in vicinity of Guadalcanal as necessary in avoiding high level bombing attack. 1147 Air raid commenced. One plane crashed into water bearing 320T. 1351 Anchored at Lunga Roads, Guadalcanal Island, Solomon Islands. 1355 Secured from General Quarters. 1412 USS TRACY moored alongside to port. 1430 Commenced fueling. 1630 Completed fueling. 1647 USS TRACY underway from alongside. 1720 Completed taking aboard 24 300-pound depth charges. 1730 Underway, join USS LITTLE and USS GREGORY. 1825 Sounded General Quarters and made preparations to meet dive bomber attack. 1915 Secured from General Quarters.

Tuesday, 1 September, 1942: 1741 Tow line secured between this vessel and WILLIAM WARD BURROWS. 1742 Commenced taking strain on towline. 1815 Hoisted anchor and took heavy strain on towline. 1835 Ceased towing operations until Burrows completed unloading.

Wednesday, 2 September, 1942: 1715 Towing wire secured to stern of GAMBLE from BURROWS. 1747 Commenced taking strain on tow wire. 1754 BURROWS pulled off Sylvia Reef by this vessel and three YP boats. 1749 Cast off towline.

Thursday, 3 September, 1942: 1545 Anchored in Tulagi Harbor astern of WILLIAM WARD BURROWS preparing to tow her clear of shoal. 1751 Secured tow line. Underway pulling BURROWS off reef. 1750 BURROWS pulled clear off reef for a second time.

Saturday, 5 September, 1942: 0055 Sighted flashes of gunfire bearing 210T. Sighted parachute flares bearing 192T. These flares were from a Navy Catalina flying boat flying over Savo Island. The pilot dropped them to illuminate what he thought was an enemy submarine. Instead the flares showed the LITTLE and GREGORY to a Japanese surface force which was close by. LITTLE and GREGORY stood no chance and were taken under fire immediately by the Japanese force. GREGORY went down at 0140 and

LITTLE about two hours later. 0548 Underway to escort BURROWS to Lunga Roads anchorage. 0735 Commenced patrolling off Lunga Roads while BURROWS and FOMALHAUT stood in to discharge cargo. Numerous landing boats to westward picking up survivors of LITTLE and GREGORY. 1105 Commenced looking for survivors of LITTLE and GREGORY. 1231 Went to General Quarters for air raid alert. 1335 Secured from GO.

Sunday, 6 September, 1942: Underway escorting WILLIAM WARD BURROWS to Espiritu Santos.

Tuesday, 10 November, 1942: Lt. G. C. Goodloe, USN reported aboard for duty.

Wednesday, 2 December, 1942: Ensign David S Stanley, USN, reported aboard for duty.

FOOTNOTE TO LOG ENTRIES - Kramer writes very plainly, easy to read. Carpenter very hard to read. Vose always prints log entries, a cinch to read. Peterson writes well. Bogart must use a pencil because the writing does not show up well. Rayburn writes well but I had a hard time figuring out what his name was from the signature.

Wednesday, 16 December, 1942: Ensign James Hector Currie III, D-V(G) USNR reported for duty aboard this vessel. (We were at anchor in Noumea, New Caledonia).

Monday, 28 December, 1942: 0630 Underway proceeding to drydock. 0727 Moored in floating drydock ARD 2. 0755 Keel is resting on the blocks. Commenced receiving electricity from the dock.

Monday, 29 November, 1943: This was a day that a draft of 10 men left the GAMBLE to Receiving Station, Espiritu Santos for further transfer to new construction. They were Barfield, Benton, Gabbert, B. V. Gentle, Dick Hansen, Haralson, Hitzfield, Jeansonn, Johnson, and Woodward. (When we got to the dock at Segond Channel and were waiting for a truck to take us to the barracks, he sniffed in the air and said, "I smell a woman." We looked around and found there was a Navy nurse standing on a high bank some 200 yards distant. What a remarkable nose he had!). We returned to the States on the USS PATTERSON (DD 392) which had her bow knocked off in a collision with the McCALLA the night of 29-30 September, 1943 near Vella Lavella. We passed under the Golden Gate Bridge at 0911, 23 December, 1943 just in time for the Christmas holidays. We were sent from Mare Island to T.I., and then off to Camp Shoemaker, near Tracy. Naturally we all wanted liberty the next morning, but they told us we were not ship's company and couldn't have liberty. We sent a delegation to each of the bases's chaplains and another to the Commanding Officer. We soon had 72-hour passes. By 31 December, 1943 we had our new assignments in hand and were granted two weeks delay in orders. Woodward and Hansen were assigned to the same ship, the USS RUDYERD BAY (CVE 81) and stayed together until the end of the war. We called Woodward "Squeaky" on the GAMBLE and that nickname stuck with him on the RUDYERD BAY.

Saturday, 25 December, 1943: Steaming as before in convoy from Suva, Fiji Islands to Purvis Bay, Florida Island, Solomon Islands.

Tuesday, 2 May, 1944: 1100 Calvo, Frank Monte MM 2/c, USN, transferred to Receiving Station, Navy 140. (Frank Montecalvo told me recently that they got his last name screwed up when he joined the Navy, and that continued all during the war. It was not until he was ready for discharge that they got it straightened out, at Frank's insistence). 1345 GAMBLE resting on blocks in ARD-5, Segond Channel, New Hebrides.

Monday, 12 June, 1944: 0810 Entered Port Jackson, Sydney, Australia. 0950 Moored port side to USS WHITNEY at Pier #2, Circular Quay.

Wednesday, 14 June, 1944: 1130 Boudreaux, Ernest Joseph, BM 1/c, USN, died of injuries sustained in a street car accident in Sydney, Australia. The investigating board found death due to unfamiliarity with local streetcar systems and not misconduct.

Friday, 16 June, 1944: Shifted ship from WHITNEY to MEDUSA.

Monday, 19 June, 1944: 1117 Underway for sea from alongside MEDUSA, Dock #2, Circular Quay, Port Jackson, Sydney, Australia.

Tuesday, 8 August, 1944: 1536 Moored starboard side to YO 161, in Tarawa Harbor.

Wednesday, 9 August, 1944: 1300 Passed into Domain of Neptunus Rex. Neptunus Rex and Court reported aboard to try, convict, and punish all trespassing "Pollywogs." 1530 Court of Neptunus Rex adjourned and Neptunus Rex, with his court, left the ship.

Saturday, 30 September, 1944: 0627 Pilot, Boatswain A. B. Cooper, USN came aboard; Captain retained the con. 0714 Moored starboard side to YO 182 at Funafuti Island Anchorage, Ellice Islands. 0940 Underway to sea by way of Buabua Channel. 1120 Sighted WIND SPOUT bearing OOOT about 5 miles from GAMBLE and bearing 330T, about 15 miles from Amatuku Island, Ellice Islands. The spout extended downward from about 1700 feet and was approximately 200 feet in diameter. At 1125, a clearly defined funnel appeared breaking off about 150 feet above the water. At 1128 spout disappeared.

Friday, 6 October, 1944: 0913 Moored port side to dock K-1, Pearl Harbor. 1318 Completed fueling ship. 1327 Shifted ship to berth alongside USS LAMBERTON.

Saturday, 7 October, 1944: 1017 Underway for Uncle Sugar Able.

Thursday, 12 October, 1944: 1608 Passed under Oakland Bay Bridge. 1654 Anchored in San Francisco Bay off Hunters Point Naval Shipyard.

Friday, 13 October, 1944: 0945 Commenced transferring ammunition and explosives to ammunition barge. 1145 Completed. 1241 Underway proceeding to Bethlehem Steel Shipyard, Alameda, California. 1345 Moored at same.

Sunday, 15 October, 1944: 1500 Cass and Peterson together with 70 enlisted personnel left for 21 days leave.

Sunday, 24 December, 1944: 2320 Moored starboard side to USS CRANE, San Diego, California.

Monday, 25 December, 1944: Christmas day in San Diego.

Sunday, 7 January, 1945: Took on fresh water, full load of fuel, and ammunition. 1723 Underway at various courses and speeds with the Captain at conn and Navigator on the bridge leaving San Diego, California for sea.

Saturday, 3 February, 1945: Moored to Buoy 8, Middle Loch, Pearl Harbor, T.H. 1355 Underway out of Pearl Harbor escorting USS CARTERET to Saipan.

Wednesday, 14 February, 1945: 1320 Maneuvering on various courses and speed to come alongside USS MOBRARA to take on fuel. Maneuvering within anchorage area of Saipan. 1750 Replogle, Raymond James, SF 2/c, transferred to receiving station, Saipan, for further transfer to US Naval Repair Base, San Diego, California. The last man to be transferred off GAMBLE before she was hit 18 February, 1945 off Iwo Jima. 1840 Left Saipan harbor heading for Iwo Jima.

Thursday, 15 February, 1945: 0000-0400 Steaming singly en route Iwo Jima on base course 340T at 173 knots. (That is what the typewritten log says - Really! - I had no idea GAMBLE could go that fast).

Saturday, 17 February, 1945: GAMBLE spent most of the day firing on various targets of opportunity on Iwo Jima as well as guarding Sweep Units 4, 5, and 6 off Iwo Jima. ⚓

SELECTED EXCERPTS FROM THE LOG OF USS GAMBLE

18 February to 16 May, 1945
Courtesy of Lieutenant Peterson

Sunday, 18 February, 1945

Steaming as before. 2010 Sent ship to General Quarters for possible air raid. 2035 Secured from General Quarters. All guns ready for immediate use. 2056 Commenced maneuvering on various courses and speeds to take station in center of formation. 2115 On Station with USS NEVADA formation. 2125 Struck by two 250 pound bombs dropped from a Japanese twin engine plane assumed to be a "Nick." Bombs struck at waterline on starboard [that crossed out and port inserted—apparently by Lt. Peterson], at bulkhead between #1 and #2 fire rooms, flooding both fire rooms. All power out, ship dead in the water.

Casualties as follows: HEAP, E. J., Blmkr 1/c, USN, missing in action. SCHUTZ, A. F., WT 2/c, USN, missing in action. DIPAOLA, E. J., F 1/c USN(I), missing in action. CAMPAGNA, S. S., F 1/c, USNR, killed in action. COONEY, H. W., WT 3/c, USNR, killed in action. The following named men were wounded: E. E. COOK, Lt(jg), USNR. H. H.MacADAMS, Jr., Ens. (SC), USNR. R. W. BOLLIER, Ens., USNR. E. B. PRITCHARD, Ens., USNR. PROKOP, J (n), S 1/c, USNR. LITZ, E. H., S 1/c, USNR. WOFFORD, J.C., Cox, USNR. LAROCCO, J (n), S 1/c, USNR. DOUBEK, R (n), Cox, USNR. LOPEZ, A (n), S 2/c, USNR.

2106 Sent ship to general quarters (this must be in error—I believe it should be 2126). Commenced shoring bulkheads and jettisoning top side ammunition and extinguishing fires. Unable to put any pumps in operation. 2130 contacted nearby ship by light in order to obtain assistance in saving ship and personnel. 2130 Fire extinguished in ready ammunition locker on galley deck house. Jettisoned 8 Mark VI depth charges. 2135 Extinguished fire in half deck. 2140 Extinguished fire in fireroom below galley. 2148 Extinguished flare up of fire on half deck. 2150 Extinguished flare up of fire in starboard side of #1 fire room. 2225 Hose from USS HAMILTON to extinguish flare up of fire in starboard side of #1 fire room. 2225 USS HAMILTON came alongside to starboard to remove wounded men. 2230 Hose from USS HAMILTON to extinguish flare up of fire on half deck and to cover oil in the fire rooms with foam. 2245 H. H. MacADAMS, Ensign, (SC), USNR, and E. E.

COOK, Lt(jg), USNR transferred in stretcher to USS HAMILTON. 2303 USS HAMILTON underway from along starboard side. 2330 Motor Whale boat from USS HAMILTON along port side. 2354 USS GAMBLE motor whale boat in the water. 2356 The remainder of the wounded men were transferred to the USS HAMILTON in the motor whale boat under the care of M. M. PARKS, Lt(jg), (MC), USN, and THOMAS, W. C., PhM 1/c, USNR.

Monday, 19 February, 1945

0000-0400 Lying dead in the water as before. 0045 CAMPAGNA, S. S., F 1/c, late of the U. S. Naval Reserve was this date committed to the deep, having been killed in action off Iwo Jima, 18 February, 1945. D. N. Clay, Comdr., USN, conducted the services. 0100 USS DORSEY alongside to starboard to take this ship in tow. 0111 Messenger out from USS DORSEY. 0126 Tow line from USS DORSEY secured to 15 fathoms of port anchor. 0142 Secured motor whale boat to stern. 0150 Underway under tow by USS DORSEY on various courses and speeds proceeding to point PAR. 0800-1200 Under tow as before. 0808 PC 800 alongside to starboard with hot coffee. 0840 PC 800 underway from along starboard side. 0845 ARS 33 standing by to render assistance. 0915 Commenced jettisoning ammunition from forward magazine. 0944 Jettisoned mast. 1000 Jettisoned ready lockers on forecastle. 1045 The following named men were transferred with bag, hammock, and records to ARS 33 for temporary duty in accordance with verbal orders from the commanding officer: (Log contains full name, serial number, rate, etc. I will list last name only) WADE, CYPERT, COPE, WIGGINTON. All hands except the following men were transferred to the ARS 33 for further transportation to SAIPAN in accordance with verbal orders from the Commanding Officer: ABBLETT, ADAMS, ASHER, BOWN, BUZZ, CAILLIER, CALHAN, COOPER, DAVIS, FOURTNER, FRANK, HENRY, JACKSON, HAYNES, KELLY, KEMP, KRANER, LEWIS, LUYSTER, MILLER, NIEDERHAUS, OLSON, PITTS, RANKIN, REYNOLDS, RUSSEL, SHEPARD, SHOGAN, SPRINGFIELD, STEWART, SULLIVAN, THOMAS, TORREY, WALKER, WILCOX, YARBROUGH, YOUNG, LATHROP, BRADLEY: Officers as follows: CLAY, PETERSON, STEWART, FLYNN, BERKELEY, CASS, VAN METRE.
1125 COONEY, H. H., WT 3/c, late of the U.S.Naval reserve was this date committed to the deep, having been killed in action off Iwo Jima, 18 February, 1945. D. N. CLAY, Comdr, USN conducted the services. 1150 completed

jettisoning ammunition having jettisoned 358 rounds of 3" 50 cal. AA common and FP, 86 rounds 3" 50 cal. armor piercing, 61 rounds of 3" 50 cal. Illum, 6 3" 50 cal. dislodging charges, 16,530 rounds of 20 MM, 25,000 50 cal., 3,000 cartridges of 30 cal., 2,000 cartridges 45 cal, 600 primers, 63 detonators.

1200-1600 Under tow as before. 1535 Jettisoned #1 stack and two 20MM guns from galley deck house. 1600-2000 Under tow as before. 1830 Darkened ship. 1940 LSM 126 alongside to starboard to take this ship in tow. 1955 Tow line transferred from USS DORSEY to LSM 126, using 1.30 fathoms of cable and 15 fathoms of chain from the port anchor. 1958 PC 800 alongside to starboard with hot soup. 2000-2400 Under tow as before. 2040 formed convoy with miscellaneous LCIs, LSMs, and AMs. OTC and guide LCI 647. Set course 205 degrees, speed 7 knots.

Tuesday, 20 February, 1945

0000-0400 Under tow by LSM 126 en route Saipan. Auxiliary power in operation. Both fire rooms flooded. 7 Officers and 39 men aboard. All hands topside. 0400-0800 0500 Motor whale boat sank and broke loose from moorings astern. Balance of day under tow.

Thursday, 21 February, 1945

1030 Jettisoned 3 inch gun from starboard side of galley deck house. 1045 Jettisoned forward boat davit. 1100 Jettisoned boat skids. Balance of day under tow for Saipan.

Thursday, 22 February, 1945

1105 Sighted two tugs bearing 180, 8 miles distant. 1130 USS MATACO alongside to take this ship in tow. 1150 Cast off tow line to LSM 126. 1240 Under tow by USS MATACO.

Sunday, 24 February, 1945

0550 Sighted SAIPAN bearing 106, distant 35 miles. 1117 Cast off tow line to USS MATACO. 1150 USS MATACO moored along starboard side with six manila lines. USS MATACO anchored in 10 fathoms of water with 30 fathoms of chain out. 1730 Under way. 1812 Taken in tow by various tugs and small craft to go alongside USS HAMUL. 1850 moored starboard side to USS HAMUL. 2000 Commenced receiving electricity and flushing water from USS HAMUL. (HAMUL AD 20) was a merchant ship converted to a Destroyer Tender).

Monday, 25 February, 1945

1300 Funeral services were held in the Marine Cemetery on SAIPAN, MARIANAS ISLANDS for the following men; DIPAOLO, E. J., F 1/c. and SCHUTZ, A. F., WT 2/c, having been killed in action off IWO JIMA, 18 February, 1945. The services were conducted by Lt.(jg), John Smith, Chaplain, USNR.

Tuesday, 26 February, 1945

0000-0004 Moored in nest with USS HAMUL in TANAPAG HARBOR, SAIPAN, MARIANAS ISLANDS, in the following order from port to starboard: LSM 126, LCI 627, USS GAMBLE, USS BLESSMAN, USS HAMUL. Receiving electricity and flushing water from USS HAMUL. 1510 Commenced receiving steam from USS HAMUL for the laundry.

Wednesday, 27 February, 1945

2300 E. B. PRITCHARD, Ensign, USNR died in U.S.ARMY Hospital #148, SAIPAN, MARIANAS ISLANDS of wounds received aboard this vessel in action off Iwo Jima, 18 February, 1945.

Thursday, 28 February, 1945

1600-2000 In accordance with orders from Commander Mine Craft, U. S. Pacific Fleet Serial 60 of 21 February, 1945, Lieutenant Richard J. Peterson, USNR, relieved Commander D. N. Clay, USN, of the duties in command of the USS GAMBLE. 1900 D. N. Clay, USN, COMINDIV II, was detached with staff from this ship. The staff consisted of the following named men: Lt(jg) P. T. King, USNR, Lt(jg) M. M. Parks(MC), USN; Springfield, H.A., YM 2/c USNR, Mayfield, C.R., StM 1/c, USNR.

Wednesday, 16 May, 1945

1245 Secured electricity and flushing water from ART 52. 1305 Underway from alongside ATR 52 proceeding out of TANAPAG HARBOR en route GUAM. 1500 ATR 52 cast off lines alongside and took this vessel in tow from ahead with 200 fathoms of 15/8" cable. ⚓

AFTER ACTION REPORT
MINING OF THE BLACKLETT STRAIT, 6 – 7 May, 1943

From: The Commander Task Group 36.5 (Commanding Officer, USS RADFORD).

To: The Commander-in-Chief, U. S. PACIFIC FLEET.

Via: (1) Commander Task Force EIGHTEEN. (2) Commander THIRD Fleet.

Subject: After Action Report of the Mining of the BLACKETT STRAIT During Nights of 6-7 May, 1943.

Reference:

(a) Commander THIRD Fleet Operation Plan 10-43 of 30 April, 1943.

(b) Commander Task Force 18 Operation Order 6-43 of 4 May, 1943.

(c) Commander Task Group 36.5 Operation order 1-43 of 3 May, 1943.

Enclosure:

(A) Track Chart of mining operations.

(B) Chart of soundings recorded by Fathometer during Mining Operations. (Original only).

1. In accordance with Commander Third Fleet Operation Plan 10-43, reference (a), as amplified by references (b) and (c), Task Group 36.5, consisting of RADFORD, PREBLE, GAMBLE, and BREESE, laid a standard three row mine field extending from 900 yards due west of MAMUTI ISLAND northward to within 1000 yards of the shore of KOLOMBANGARA ISLAND in the vicinity of VANGAVANGA. The sea was moderate, the sky was overcast with intermittent extremely heavy rain squalls, and no moon. Visibility was fair to absolutely zero in squalls. The approach,

squalls, and no moon. Visibility was fair to absolutely zero in squalls. The approach, the mining, and the retirement were carried out in accordance with plan set forth in my Operation Order 1-43.

2. Narrative: Task Group 36.5, consisting of RADFORD, PREBLE, GAMBLE, and BREESE, departed ESPIRITU SANTO at 1700 Love on 4 May, 1943 en route TULAGI HARBOR, FLORIDA ISLAND, at 17 knots, via points X-ray, Yoke and SEALARK CHANNEL. Held three rehearsal runs simulating actual courses and mining formation to be taken for scheduled operation. Two runs were made at night and one during daylight. Last rehearsal run made at night proved highly satisfactory and all ships had perfect confidence that station-keeping and maneuver could be accomplished according to plan.

On 3 May, 1943 a Raytheon Company representative accompanied by an officer radar representative made two alterations to the SG radar on RADFORD but were unable to tune the set properly in harbor due to land effect. During the passage from ESPIRITU SANTO to TULAGI the SG radar failed to function properly in spite of the constant effort of the chief radar technician to improve performance. Finally as a last resort the "gaiting" alteration was removed and the set then functioned in a highly satisfactory manner. Since the success of the entire operation hinged on proper functioning of radar this incident caused the Commanding Officer unnecessary anxiety and concern.

The Task Group arrived at TULAGI at 1000 Love on 6 May and fueled from the ERSKINE PHELPS. During fueling the condition was "Red" over the RUSSELLS but the condition remained "Green" at TULAGI.

The Approach: Task Group 3g.5 departed at 1330 from TULAGI and passed through initial point Lat. 09° 10' S., Long. 159° 35' E. at 1600 Love on course 244° T. at 26 knots. At 1416 GAMBLE reported leaky boiler tube in one boiler but able to make 27 knots. At 1700 Love changed course to 284° T. At 1910 radar contact was made on a plane with doubtful IFF, bearing 105° T., distance 27 miles. This plane passed up starboard side of formation at 3600 yards distance. Positive IFF was not obtained until the plane passed ahead. It has since been established by conversation with cruiser spotters that this was a Black Cat plane which did not become aware of presence of Task Group until practically overhead. It must again be emphasized that this practice of the aviators is disconcerting to surface forces and dangerous to themselves. At 2130 Love changed course to 324° T. At 2300 Love changed speed to 15 knots. Fixes were obtained by radar en route to NEW GEORGIA and RENDOVA ISLANDS. Excellent results were obtained and SINBO ISLAND was clearly distinguishable at 58,000 yards on SG screen. Estimate of time schedule was five minutes slow. Speeds, however, were maintained according to plan to prevent straggling. At 2325 changed course to 034° T. At 2327 changed course to 030° T. Radar indicated that right hand reef off west end of WANAWANA ISLAND was approximately 500 to 700 yards further to the westward, making the entrance 2300 yards wide instead of 3000 yards as charted. The passage through the reef was made entirely by radar and sound plots. Right and left hand tangents of the landmass on each side of the passage were used in the case of radar and these were constantly checked by the starboard and port sound gears ranging on the right and left reefs respectively. Intermittent views of the various islands were seen from the bridge and what visual bearings were possible were taken and passed to the Combat Information Center. The fact that these few visual bearings checked exactly with radar plot afforded the Commanding Officer and the Executive Officer in C.I.C. some assurance that all was going well. At 2340 the Task Group entered squally weather with low to zero visibility. At 2358, while in the center of FERGUSON PASSAGE, there was a deluge of rain with absolute zero visibility. At 0004 with above zero visibility the following TBS transmissions without preliminary call ups were made: 0004 BREESE "Request a mark on commencement." 0004 RADFORD "Wilco, Wilco." 0004 GAMBLE "Repeat Please." 0005 RADFORD "Mark. I am turning. That is all." This unauthorized transmission by the BREESE is understandable in view of visibility conditions.

The Mining Operation: At 0005 RADFORD changed to mining course 000° T. with MAKUTI ISLAND 900 yards on the starboard beam bearing 120° T. The PREBLE followed in the RADFORD's wake and as the PREBLE turned, the GAMBLE and BREESE turned simultaneously with her to the mining course. Mining was started in the turn and completed on time at the end of an 8400-yard run. Mining speed was 15 knots, mining interval 12 seconds (100 yards), mining time 17 minutes.

While in the initial turn to the mining course, visibility cleared sufficiently to show the formation and it was heartening to see that all ships were in perfect position, in spite of only intermittent visual contact for approximately 10-15 minutes. During the major portion of the run on mining course, visibility was fair. At 0018 RADFORD changed course to 340° T. in order to parallel the shoreline of KOLOMBANGARA ISLAND at 1000 yards. At 0019 RADFORD made sound contact on 315° T., distance 1500 yards. This contact could not be duplicated by radar nor could anything be seen visually. The presence of a shoal was feared but this anxiety was eased when sound reported the contact as a reciprocal echo from the beach on our starboard quarter. During the change to course 340° T., the PREBLE followed in wake of RADFORD, while GAMBLE and BREESE maintained approximate station. Resultant minefield is as shown in Track Chart (Enclosure A).

The Retirement: At 0020 RADFORD changed course to 310° T. and simultaneously there was an intense squall with wind force 7. At 0022 increased speed to 27 knots and turned on ABE equipment to aid Task Force 18 in establishing recognition. All ships of Task Group 36.5 formed column. At 0022 radar shifted to long scale and made excellent radar contact on Task Force 18 bearing 346°, distance 21,000 yards. SG scope showed exact formation and plot checked accurately on scheduled course and speed. At 0035 changed course to 000° T. At 0051 changed course to 050°. At 0102 changed course to 060° T. to commence easing in ahead of Task Force 18. At 0106 changed course to 070° T. At 0119 changed course to 090° T. At 0130 secured ABE. At 0216 sighted flare astern. At 0245 changed course to 120° T. and continued retirement on this course. At daybreak GAMBLE and BREESE reported unable to make scheduled speed and return to ESPIRITU SANTO without fueling. At 0758 Task Group was ordered by Commander Task Force 18 to proceed to TULAGI for fuel and proceeded independently to TULAGI. At 0948 arrived and fueled. At 1252 departed for ESPIRITU SANTO via LENGO CHANNEL and points Yoke and X-ray at 24 knots. At 0555 contacted Task Force 18. RADFORD joined Task Force EIGHTEEN and PREBLE (Comtask Unit 36.5.2) with BREESE and GAMBLE proceeded independently for ESPIRITU SANTO.

3. Comments:

(a) Rehearsal runs were found necessary and proved extremely helpful.

(b) A great deal of worry and anxiety were experienced because of poor performance of SG radar after alteration and prior to repair.

(d) Continuous drill of C. I. C. in coordinating SG, FD and sound information was well repaid in the assurance that was obtainable from this information in the passage through FERGUSON PASSAGE and the close approach to KOLOMBANGARA, each of which was made under zero visibility. At no time did the Executive Officer of the RADFORD, acting as coordinator, lack accurate and continuous information and assurance that "all was well."

(e) No reports of enemy contacts were received from Black Cat planes furnishing reconnaissance for Task Group 36.5.

(f) The minelayers kept excellent station in spite of the poor to absolutely zero visibility.

(g) The minefield was laid without a single premature explosion and, from Comairsols dispatch to Comtaskgroup 36.5 of the daylight air report of reconnaissance, without a single "floater."

(h) It is believed that the operation was accomplished in total ignorance to the enemy primarily due to the extremely heavy and timely squalls. No action was necessary and none was taken by the Task Group that might have disclosed their presence. The short TBS transmissions at 0004 were unauthorized by the Operation Order but are believed excusable under the adverse conditions of weather.

(i) The success of the operation is conclusively evidenced by the reports of coast watchers which reveal that enemy ships of both combatant and non-combatant types have been sunk in the mine field within 48 hours of laying.

(j) It is felt that in spite of the fact that the operation was carried out "without incident," it was still a highly commendable performance. The anxiety, anticipation, and worry preceding and during an operation of this type were all present and the successful accomplishment under these stresses merely amplifies the good work that was done. Each ship and each officer and man did his duty and are highly commended by this command.

4. It is considered that the Commanding Officers of the PREBLE, GAMBLE, and BREESE are worthy of praise for the excellent station keeping and sterling performance of their respective ships during the approach, mining operation and retirement. Likewise the Executive Officer of the U.S.S. RADFORD, Lieutenant Commander William H. Groverman, U.S.N., who as Evaluating Officer in the Combat Intelligence Center, is deserving of especial praise for his superlative work in navigating the Task Group under adverse and trying circumstances. Likewise Pratice, Lawrence (n), #393 10 87, CRT(AA), is deserving of praise for his proficiency in restoring the SG radar of this vessel to proficient operating condition.

5. The matter of appropriate awards for outstanding performance of duty by individuals during the conduct of this operation will be made the subject of separate correspondence.

W. M. ROMOSER

Distribution:

Advance Copies: Cominch U.S. Fleet Cincpac Fleet Com. Third Fleet ⚓

COMMENDATIONS:

MAY 7, 1943

FROM: COMMANDER TASK UNIT 36.5
TO: TASK UNIT 36.5
MY CONGRATULATIONS ON A HAZARDOUS MISSION
ABLY AND WELL DONE BT 062257

MAY 14, 1943

NOTICE TO ALL HANDS:
COMSOPAC HAS SENT A MESSAGE CONGRATULATING THE CRUISERS
AND MINE FORCE ON ANOTHER GREAT PERFORMANCE.
HE ADDED THAT IT WAS BECOMING A HABIT FOR THESE GROUPS.

W. W. ARMSTRONG
LIEUTENANT COMMANDER, USN COMMANDING

MAY 9, 1943

ACCORDING TO THE LATEST REPORTS WE HAVE, OUR
MINE FIELD HAD ALREADY KNOCKED OFF TWO AK'S (FREIGHTERS)
AND ONE DESTROYER. SOME MORE DESTROYERS ARE ALSO
REPORTED AS BEING INVOLVED IN THE FIELD TODAY. WE WILL ADD
THESE TO OUR GROWING GROUP ON THE WINGS OF THE BRIDGE
WHEN FULL REPORTS ARE RECEIVED.

W. W. ARMSTRONG
LIEUTENANT COMMANDER, USN COMMANDING

I thought you might like to have a copy of this commendation to let you know what we have been doing and to tell you that I give the credit to the members of the crew for making runs like this possible.

W. W. Armstrong

———

SOUTH PACIFIC FORCE OF THE UNITED STATES PACIFIC FLEET HEADQUARTERS OF THE COMMANDER

The Commander South Pacific Area and South Pacific Force takes pleasure in commending

LIEUTENANT COMMANDER WARREN WILSON ARMSTRONG, UNITED STATES NAVY

for service as set forth in the following CITATION:

"For skillful and effective performance of duty in the line of his profession as Commanding Officer of a fast mine layer on two successful mining missions into enemy waters. On the night of May 6-7, 1943, a detachment of light mine layers of which Lieutenant Commander ARMSTRONG's vessel was a unit, made a difficult approach through restricted waters in total darkness into Blackett Strait, Solomon Islands, and laid an effective mine field, undetected by the enemy, to within a thousand yards of an enemy held coast line. This mine field took a toll of enemy combatant and non-combatant ships within forty-eight hours. Again, on the night of May 12-13, 1943, the same detachment, in perfect coordination with a bombardment of enemy shore positions and installations by a surface task force, laid an effective mine field to within a thousand yards of an enemy-held coast line in Kula Gulf, Solomon Islands. The success of both the operations was largely due to the intrepidity and professional skill of Lieutenant Commander ARMSTRONG. His conduct throughout was in keeping with the highest traditions of the United States Naval Service."

W. F. HALSEY,
Admiral, US Navy.

AFTER ACTION REPORT
MINING OF EAST COAST OF KOLOMBANGARA
ISLAND, 12 -13 May, 1943

From: The Commander Task Group 36.5 (Commanding Officer USS RADFORD).

To: The Commander-in-Chief, U. S. Pacific Fleet.

Via: (1) The Commander Task Force EIGHTEEN. (2) The Commander THIRD Fleet.

Subject: Mining of East Coast of KOLOMBANGARA ISLAND in Vicinity of OKOPO RIVER During Night of 12-13 May, 1943; Action report of.

Reference:
(a) Commander THIRD Fleet Operation Plan 11-43 of 7 May, 1943.
(b) Commander Task Force EIGHTEEN Operation Order 7-43 of 9 May, 1943.
(c) Commander Task Group 36.5 Operation Order 2-43 of 9 May, 1943.

Enclosure:
(A) Track Chart of Mining Operations.
(B) Chart of Soundings Recorded by Fathometer During Mining Operations. (Original Only)

1. In accordance with Commander THIRD Fleet Operation Plan 11-43, (reference (a)), as amplified by reference (b) and (c), Task Group 36.5 Consisting of RADFORD, PREBLE, GAMBLE, and BREESE, laid a standard three row mine field extending from a point 1000 Bards due east of the mouth of the OKOPO RIVER on a line of bearing of 110 T. for a distance of 8400 yards. The sea was calm, the sky was partly overcast, the moon had set prior to commencing the mining operation, the night was dark, and the visibility good. The approach, the mining, and the retirement were carried out without incident in accordance with plan set forth in my Operation Order 2-43.

2. Narrative: Task Group 36.5 departed ESPIRITU SANTO at 1700 Love on 10 May, 1943 en route TULAGI HARBOR, FLORIDA ISLAND at 17 knots via points XRAY, YOKE, and SEALARK CHANNEL. Held two rehearsal runs en route simulating actual courses and mining formation to be taken for scheduled operation. One rehearsal run was made during daylight and one at night. At 2155 Love 10 May RADFORD made radar contact which proved on investigation to be small coastal vessel. At 0610 Love 12 May contacted air coverage in vicinity of NURA ISLAND. At 1000 Love arrived TULAGI and entire Task Group fueled from ERSKINE PHELPS which had bare minimum fuel available for Task Force EIGHTEEN north of SAVO ISLAND. Task Force sighted in vicinity of SEALARK CHANNEL while proceeding out of TULAGI. At 1630 Love formed column astern of Task Force EIGHTEEN on base course 3000 T. at 20 knots. At 1706 Love changed speed to 21 knots. At 1801 BREESE reported blower casualty reducing maximum speed to 25 knots. At 1825 Love passed through Lat. 8° 50' S. Long. 159° 25' E. on course 300 T. at 25 knots. Proceeding in accordance with Annex Baker of Commander Task Group EIGHTEEN Operation Order 7-43. Approach was uneventful except for numerous contacts made on friendly planes considered to be Black Cats. During approach visibility was excellent with a new moon silhouetting the force too effectively for comfort. At 0018 Love Task Group 36.5 proceeded independently on various courses and speeds to reach a point 1000 yards off the mouth of the OKOPO RIVER. At 0056 Love sighted searchlights at VILA Airfield. At 0057 Love at a point 1000 yards east of the OKOPO RIVER changed course to 110° T at 15

knots and commenced mining operations. At 0101 Love cruisers commenced firing. At 0116 changed course to 041° T. and increased speed to 25 knots - mining operations completed. Made retirement in accordance with plan. At 0258 sighted fire on NICHOLAS caused by casualty to No. 3 gun. At 0525 Love sighted red light, believed running light of plane, bearing 310° T. At 0528 Love light identified as friendly plane. At 0530 Love HONOLULU reported plane as friendly. At 0534 STRONG commenced firing. At 0535 STRONG ceased firing. At 0558 Task Unit 36.5.2, on orders from Comtaskfor 18, left formation and proceeded independently to TULAGI for fuel. RADFORD (Task Unit 36.5.1) joined destroyer screen for Task Force EIGHTEEN.

3. The mining operation was executed in exact accordance with plan. No opposition was received from the beach, and there were no indications that the minelaying was detected by the enemy.

4. All personnel of Task Group 36.5 conducted themselves with calmness and efficiency and are to be congratulated upon their fine performance of duty. The Commanding Officers of PREBLE, BREESE, and GAMBLE are to be commended for the excellent manner in which their ships kept station on RADFORD during the approach, and for the proficient handling of their respective ships during the mining operation.

W. M. ROMOSER

Distribution: Advance Copies: Cominch U.S.Fleet Cincpac Fleet Com. Third Fleet

Copies: Comdesron 21 Comdespac Comairsopac ⚓

82

COMMENDATIONS

JUNE 30, 1943
FROM: COMMANDER TASK GROUP 36.2.2
TO: GAMBLE, BREESE, PREBLE

-T-A- 6122 292100 M65 M 68 M70 GR 25 BT
PLEASE ACCEPT MY THANKS ADMIRATION AND COMMENDATION TO ALL
OFFICERS AND MEN ON THE GAMBLE, BREESE, AND PREBLE. FOR THE
EXCELLENT WORK DONE LAST NIGHT BT 292100. ADMIRAL HALSEY SAYS HE
IS PROUD OF US AND CONGRATULATES THE FORCE ON A HAZARDOUS JOB
WELL DONE.
　　　　　　W. W. ARMSTRONG LIEUTENANT COMMANDER, USN COMMANDING.

JUNE 30, 1943
FROM: COMMANDER TASK GROUP 36.2
TO: GAMBLE, BREESE, PREBLE

-T-A- M65 -A- 612 300045 M65 M68 M70 GR 25 BT
DUTY COMPLETED X WELL DONE X I CONGRATULATE YOU ON A BIG JOB
PERFECTLY EXECUTED X YOU ARE A STOUT LOT X KEEP IT UP BT 300045
　　　　　　　　　　　　　W. W. ARMSTRONG

JULY 4, 1943
FROM: COMSOPAC (COMMANDER SOUTH PACIFIC)
TO: GAMBLE, BREESE, PREBLE.

-T-A- 0F3 041953 M65 M68 M70 GR 23 BT YOU HAVE DONE A GRAND JOB AGAIN
IN CARRYING WAR TO THE JAPS X AWARD CONGRATULATIONS TO ALL
HANDS ON BOARD X HALSEY   BT 041953

THE TASK FORCE COMMANDER WISHES TO ADD HIS APPRECIATION TO THE
CONGRATULATIONS ALREADY RECEIVED FROM ADMIRAL HALSEY FOR THE
SUCCESS OF YOUR RECENT OPERATIONS AGAINST THE ENEMY. ESPECIAL
CREDIT IS DUE TO THE GAMBLE, BREESE AND PREBLE, ABLY LED BY
RADFORD, FOR THE WAY THEY PRINTED W-E-L-C-O-M-E ON THE JAP DOOR
MAT. THE CRUISERS AND DESTROYERS HAVE AGAIN DEMONSTRATED THAT
THE JAPS CAN'T HANDLE OUR PITCHING, EVERY OFFICER AND MAN SHOULD
HAVE A JUST PRIDE IN KNOWING THAT BOTH JOBS WERE INDEED "WELL
DONE."
　　　　　　　　　　　　W. L. AINSWORTH ⚓

REPORT OF MINELAYING OPERATION

November 2, 1943

TO: GAMBLE, BREESE, PREBLE

From: Commander Task Unit 31.8.1 Commanding Officer USS RENSHAW (DD-499).

To: The Chief of Naval Operations.

Via: (1) Commander Task Force THIRTY-ONE
  (2) Commander Third Fleet
  (3) Commander-in-Chief, U.S.Pacific Fleet (4) Commander-in-Chief, U. S. Fleet

Subject: Minelaying Operation; Report of.

Enclosure: (A) Overlay of Chart showing Mine Field.

1. In accordance with reference (c), the completion of minelaying operations directed by reference (a) is reported. Task Unit 31.8.1 consisting of RENSHAW (DD499), BREESE (DM 18), SICARD (DM 21) and GAMBLE (DM15) departed Latitude 06° 47' S, Longitude 154° 36' E at 2100 L, 1 November, 1943 and maneuvered thereafter as indicated in enclosure (A). Task Force 39 covered the Minelaying Unit against surface opposition.

2. A three-line mine field was laid. The point of origin of northern row is 3,000 yards bearing 160° T from Cape Moltke, Bougainville Island. The field runs on course 250° T from point of origin. Distance between rows of mines is 400 yards.

There are 85 mines in each row. The two northern rows are 4 miles in length and the mines are evenly spaced. The first 75 mines of the southern row are laid in accordance with standard procedure. The last 10 mines of this row are unevenly spaced due to mine track jams. The length of the southern row of mines is slightly more than 6 miles. The location of those mines is shown in the enclosure.

3. Navigation was by Sugar George radar. The location of the field is believed to be accurately established.

4. The mines were received from the Naval Mine Depot, Espiritu Santos, New Hebrides, and were equipped as follows:

  Mines: 255, Mark VI
  Case Depth: 30 feet
  Float Depth: 10 feet
  Anchor depth: 500 fathoms
  Float release: 10 - 12 feet K2, Mod. 2, with Anti-paravane device removed.
  Vane unlocking depth: 15 feet.
  Safety switch arming device: 15 feet. Mark VI Booster
  Detonator: Mark I, Mod. I Extender: 13 - 15 feet Dash pot: 8 - 11 sec. Hold off
    nut: 4 turns
  Washer: Green 3 - 9 hour delay
  Has extra H6 horn on top of float
  Float Release mechanism, Mark 3, Mod. 2
  No sterilizers
  There were no prematures.

5. The minefield was laid in poorly charted waters. Until the final leg, a speed of 10 knots was maintained. With the ship in a least a depth of 50 fathoms, echoes on shoals were obtained between latitudes 060° 14' S and 060° 18' S at longitude 154° 47' E. Depth of water over these shoals is unknown as the Unit was maneuvered to clear them. The approach course was 340° T, approach and laying speed 15 knots.

6. The night was bright with starlight. While on the approach course, a twin-engine bomber picked up the formation. A little later, a float plane also picked up the formation. Both planes were in the area for about 5 minutes after which time the bomber was not seen again. The float plane dropped float lights and flares during the mining. It is doubtful that this plane realized that mines were being laid. There was no evidence of life on the beach.

7. During withdrawal, Task Force 39 very effectively covered the Mine Laying Unit. Shortly after passing to the eastward of Task Force 39, this force picked up a surface contact to the westward. Task Force 39 fought a night engagement with the enemy within view and TBS range of this Unit. This Unit cleared the scene of action as expeditiously as possible (26 knots) but was confined to a southerly course on account of the Transports returning to Torokina being to the eastward of this Unit and shoal water being to the eastward of the Transports. Fortunately this Unit did not embarrass Task Force 39. Had this Unit been about an hour later along its track, there would not have been too much sea room for anyone.

J. A. LARK ⚓

USS GAMBLE, November 2, 1943 NOTICE TO ALL HANDS:

The planes dropping flares on us last night were Japanese twin float seaplanes and operating in conjunction with an enemy task force standing down the Southern coast of Bougainville. Very shortly after our completion of mining, this enemy group was engaged in a night surface encounter by a task force of ours consisting of cruisers and destroyers. Some of our ships were damaged but all are still afloat. Total damage to the Japs is unknown at present, but it is known that the remaining Japs retired northward after the encounter.

Without the support of our cruisers and destroyers, our group of minelayers would have been in a serious situation on the retirement from the mine planting. We are all happy because of the timely arrival of our own task force and the presence of those some odd fifteen minutes we had to spare.

The Captain wants to congratulate all hands on their excellent conduct during the mine planting and particularly for their calmness and attention to duty while our yellow friends were making us look like old time Broadway at night.

W.W. ARMSTRONG LIEUTENANT COMMANDER, USN COMMANDING

November 10, 1943. USS Gamble
EXCERPT FROM RADIO PRESS NEWS, OF INTEREST TO ALL HANDS.

The following is quoted from a report by Admiral Merrill on our mine laying operations off the Shortlands on the 29th and 30th of June, 1943:

"EACH OF THESE SHIPS CARRIED 84 MINES AND IT WAS NOT DESIRED TO UNDULY HAZARD THEM IN A GUNNERY ACTION. UNFORTUNATELY THEY HAD TO BE STATIONED AHEAD TO SET THE PACE. BECAUSE OF THEIR AGE AND THEIR HEAVY MINE LOADS THERE WAS SOME QUESTION OF THEIR BEST SUSTAINED SPEED, AND ALSO THE POSSIBILITY OF A BREAKDOWN. OUR SUSPICIONS WERE ENTIRELY UNJUSTIFIED. NOT ONLY DID THEY MAINTAIN A CONSTANT SPEED OF 26 KNOTS EN ROUTE TO SHORTLANDS, WHICH PERMITTED THE BOMBARDMENT TO START WITHIN TWO MINUTES OF THE TIME PREDICTED, BUT THEY RETURNED THE ENTIRE DISTANCE OF 300 MILES AT AN AVERAGE SPEED OF 27 KNOTS."

(THE COMMANDER IN CHIEF OF THE U.S. FLEET MAKES THIS REMARK TO THE ABOVE STATEMENT: "GREAT CREDIT IS DUE TO THE OFFICERS AND MEN OF THESE MINE-LAYERS IN MAINTAINING THESE TWENTY-FIVE-YEAR-OLD SHIPS IN OPERATING CONDITION").

"THE TASK GROUP COMMANDER CONSIDERS THAT THE MINING UNIT DID A REMARKABLY FINE PIECE OF WORK. THE UNIT COMMANDER IN THE PRINGLE, WITH HER SC RADAR, DID AN EXCELLENT PIECE OF NAVIGATION, AND THE MINE LAYERS DISPLAYED SUPURB SEAMANSHIP IN ACTUALLY MAINTAINING THEIR FORMATION IN ROUGH WATER DURING CONDITIONS OF ALMOST ZERO VISIBILITY AND WHILE MAKING RADICAL COURSE AND SPEED CHANGES ON CLOCK WITHOUT SIGNAL."

(THE COMMANDER IN CHIEF COMMENTS AS FOLLOWS: "THESE SHIPS CONTINUE TO MAINTAIN THEIR HIGH STANDARD AS EVIDENCED BY THIS AND PREVIOUS OPERATIONS").

W.W. ARMSTRONG, LIEUT-COMDR U.S.N. COMMANDING

Christmas and New Year's Greetings to All Relatives of the Crew from the USS GAMBLE

As Commanding Officer and therefore a representative of the entire crew, I send you best wishes for the Holiday Season and for the coming year. Although your loved one will be unable to be with you this year, I know
that his thoughts are of his home these days, for along with our Christmas wishes we all hold close the thoughts of our future peacetime lives.

That this day of normal livelihood will inevitably return is evident by the work of all hands during these fighting days. I can vouch for the outstanding work of all members of this ship's company. By their excellent work they have carried the ship through crucial situations and gained for it and themselves a reputation for smartness and toughness.

You by your letter writing can keep your son, husband or brother close to his home, near to the things that are dear to him, and ready for his future normal life, thereby helping to maintain the spirit that is the very life blood of a fighting ship.

May we all look forward to the return of the days "Of Peace on Earth, Good Will to Men."

W. W. ARMSTRONG
Lieutenant Commander, U. S. Navy Commanding
(CHRISTMAS DAY 1943)

GAMBLE'S LAST VOYAGE

As recorded in the INDUSTRIAL NEWS, A mimeographed newsletter published by the Naval Operating Base, GUAM, M.I., 27 July, 1945 (Courtesy of Bob Kraner)

Many of you here at the Industrial Department have worked salvaging material from the old DD berthed at #2 dock. Aboard the ship working on the decks, in the holds, the shattered engine rooms, amid the wreckage and debris, green-clad sailors were busily engaged in dismantling the salvageable material from the battered hulk, hit by bombs off the coast of Iwo Jima. The remains of the once proud man of war were being salvaged for re-use on other more fortunate ships of the fleet.

The GAMBLE was built and commissioned in 1918 at Norfolk, Virginia, a four stacker, and one of the speediest ships of her type. In 1930, GAMBLE was converted into the DM 15 and kept her original name, which suited her fate.

Sunday, 15 July at 1300, one could observe a group of men lowering canvas-covered bags into the holds of the GAMBLE. The bags held charges of Tetratol. The loading continued until the ship held one and a half tons of the powerful explosive. Then the men of the Underwater Demolition Team #19 strung long lines of fuse about the deck, the last crew to board the gallant GAMBLE.

At 1415, the GAMBLE, towed by YTB-381, left on her last voyage. On the tug were correspondents representing the U.S. and South American press as well as photographers from all the syndicates. As the sad procession passed out of the harbor, perhaps the sailors of the proud ships in the bay paused in their work and watched, wondering about the fate of their stricken comrade. Perhaps they reflected on their own uncertain future. It was a tribute to the GAMBLE, and to the lost men of her crew, that those who watched straightened to attention and saluted as the broken hulk was towed to her watery grave.

The procession continued on out to sea for about eight miles, and at a signal blast from the tug, halted. The Officer signaled to the crew aboard the ship. They made last minute checks, and set the fuses for 15 minutes. Then the crew aboard GAMBLE debarked, boarded the tug, and she moved off a distance of 500 yards.

The GAMBLE wallowed in the seas, a lonesome figure with a proud name, and a history to be written in the annals of the world's greatest Navy.

As the cameramen ground away and the reporters took final notes, the final explosion in the violent life of the GAMBLE took place. The stern lifted slightly in the air as thousands of pieces of debris rained on the sea. Then the stern suddenly dipped and the bow rose. Slowly, and proudly, the ship slid beneath the waves. ⚓

The *Gamble* after being severely damaged in February, 1945. Deemed unfit for further service after taking a Japanese bomb directly down the funnel, *Gamble*, once a four-pipe destroyer, became a victim of euthanasia. Towed several miles to sea on 16 July off Apra Harbor, Oran, she blew sky high from TNT in the stern and sank in one minute. Though doomed, the hulk distributed some of the personal effects of her former crew members over a wide area. She's down 3000 fathoms.

Down Went the Gamble [DM-15] Standish Backus #9 Watercolor, 1945 88-186-I

A PARTIAL LIST OF OFFICERS WHO SERVED ABOARD THE USS GAMBLE (DM-15)

With dates aboard, if known. I do not have a complete copy of the log of the GAMBLE, and that is the only source of that information. The information contained in this list came from a few pages of the GAMBLE log sent to me by Lieutenant R J Peterson, the last Commanding Officer. Commanding Officers not listed except in the case of Lt. Peterson.

From log dated 1 July, 1942

SMITH, M.J., Lieutenant - 6/30/40 - Exec
BOGART, F.L., Lieutenant - 7/26/40 - Gunnery, Mining, Ships Serv.
CARPENTER, R.E., Lieutenant (jg) - 1/3/41 - Engineering, Damage Control
CALHOUN, H.W., Lieutenant (jg) - 3/14/41 - Communications
RAYBURN, J.H. Jr., Lieutenant (jg) - 1/21/41 - 1st Lt
VOSE, W.R., Ensign - 1/19/42 - Ass't S.C. & Sound Officer
KRAMER, E.J., Ensign - 4-28-42 - Ass't Eng & Commisary Officer
PETERSON, R.J., Ensign - 7/2/42 - Ass't Gunnery, Ass't Damage Control

From Log of 1 December, 1943

CARPENTER, R.E., Lieutenant - 1/3/41
GEISE, ?. G., Lieutenant - ????
PETERSON, R. J. Lieutenant - 7/2/42
BERKELEY, H. C., Ensign - 7/20/43
CURRIE, J.H., III, Ensign
GARFINKLE, MAX G., Ensign - Died at Tulagi, September, 1944 from virus infection.
FLYNN, C.J., Ensign - 7/20/43
GITTLER, L., Ensign - ?
CASS, WILLIAM H., Ensign - 11/11/43
VAN METRE, B.H., Ensign - 11/11/43

From Log of 1 October, 1944

CARPENTER, R.E., LIEUTENANT - 1/3/41	Exec & Navigator
STEWART, E.R., Lieutenant - 6/13/44	Ass't Navigator
PETERSON, R.J., Lieutenant - 7/2/42	Engineering Officer
CURRIE, J.H., III, Lieutenant (jg) - 12/16/42	Comm. Officer
FLYNN, C.J., Lieutenant (jg) - 7/20/43	Gunnery Officer
BERKELEY, H.C.Jr., Lieutenant (jg) - 7/20/43	Radar-Sonar Officer
CASS, W.H. Jr., Ensign - 11/11/43	Ass't Comm & Signal Officer
VAN METRE, B.H., Ensign - 11/11/43	Ship Repair & Ass't Comm.
BOLLIER.R.W., Ensign - 7/20/44	1st Lt. & Mining Officer
PARKS,M.M., Lieutenant (jg) - 8/30/44	Medical Officer

From Log of 1 December, 1944

PETERSON, R.J., Lieutenant -	Executive Officer
STEWART, E.R., Lieutenant -- 6/13/44	Engineering Officer
FLYNN, C.J., Lt.(jg) - 7/20/43	Gunnery Officer
KNUDSON, C.C., Lt. (jg) - 11/10/44	Radar/Sonar Officer
BERKELEY, H.C., Jr., Lt(jg) - 7/20/43	Navigator
CASS, W.H., Jr., Lt.(jg)	Communications Officer
VAN METRE, B.H., Lt.(jg) - 11/11/43 1st Lt	Ships Repair
McADAMS, H.H., Ensign - 11/10/44	Disbursing
BOLLIER, R.W., Ensign - 7/20/44	Mining & Depth Charge Officer
PRITCHARD,E.B., Ensign - 11/10/44	Ass't Eng
RADER, R.F., Ensign - 12/6/44	Ass't Comm

Added to 1 December list for 1 February, 1945

COOK, E.E., Lt(jg) - 1/16/45	Mine Officer

COOK, BOLLIER, and McADAMS were wounded the night of 18 February, 1945 and transferred to hospital that date. PRITCHARD was transferred to a hospital or hospital ship (date not clear in log) and died in the hospital at Saipan, 28 February, 1945.

Log for 1 March, 1945

PETERSON, R.J., Lieutenant	Commanding Officer
STEWART, E.R., Lieutenant	Executive Officer
FLYNN, C.J., Lt.(jg)	Gunnery Officer
KNUDSON, C.C., Lt.(jg)	Radar/Sonar Officer
BERKELEY, H.C.,Jr., Lt.(jg)	Navigator
CASS, W.H., Lt.(jg)	Communications Officer
VAN METRE, B.H., Lt.(jg)	First Lieutenant
RADER, R.F., Ensign	Ass't Comm. Officer

Bronze plaques were installed on Saipan at the graves of the following men by crew members of the USS GAMBLE:

Ernest J. DiPaulo Fl/c 869 90 21, killed in action off Iwo Jima 18 February, 1945.

Albert F. Schutz WT 2/c 2875944, born 6 December 1924. Killed in action off Iwo Jima 18 February, 1945.

Elbert B. Pritchard, Ensign USNR 359468. Born 14 August 1922, died at Saipan 27 February 1945 as a result of injuries sustained aboard the USS Gamble on 18 February 1945 in the battle for Iwo Jima.

They went with songs to the battle, they were young.

Straight of limb, true of eyes, steady and aglow.

They were staunch to the end against odds uncounted,

They fell with their faces to the foe.

They shall grow not old, as we that are left grow old:

Age shall not weary them, nor the years condemn.

At the going down of the sun and in the morning,

We will remember them.

They mingle not with their laughing comrades again;

They sit no more at familiar tables of home;

They have no lot in our labor of the daytime;

They sleep beyond America's foam.

A ROSTER OF ALL THE ENLISTED MEN WHO SERVED ON THE USS GAMBLE (DM-15) FROM 25 SEPTEMBER 1939 THROUGH 1 JUNE 1945

The following men were killed in action on 18 February 1945, when the GAMBLE got hit with two bombs from a Japanese plane at Iwo Jima:

CAMPAGNA, Salvadore S., F 1/c - enlisted 10 June, 1943, San Francisco, CA and came to GAMBLE 1 February, 1944.

COONEY, Harold W., WT-3/c - enlisted 10 May, 1943, Springfield, MA, came to GAMBLE on 1 February, 1944.

DIPAOLA, Earnest James, F 2/c - enlisted 5 May, 1943, Minneapolis, MN, came to GAMBLE 14 August, 1943.

SCHUTZ, Albert F., WT 2/c, enlistment not known, when to GAMBLE not known.

The following sailor was lost at sea the same night and is listed as "Lost at sea in line of duty":

HEAP, Edwin John, Blmkr 1/c - enlisted 16 December, 1941, New Orleans, LA, to GAMBLE 26 January, 1942.

The following symbols are used following names to signify they were aboard during a certain event:

\# Aboard in 1939, making them part of the original crew after GAMBLE was recommissioned.
& Aboard 7 December, 1941, when the Japanese attacked Pearl Harbor.
* Aboard when the GAMBLE was hit at Iwo Jima.

KEY TO IDENTIFICATION

Name   Date Came Aboard   Date Left   Rate at Those Respective Times

Abblett, Walter D * 12-2-40, 6-1-45, AS CGM

Abbott, Harold G, Jr. 5-4-42, 3-25-44, AS S 1/c

Adams, Charles W # & * 9-25-39, 6-1-45, AS CMM

Adcox, Harold L * 1-26-45, 5-14-45, S 2/c S 1/c

Albersmeyer, Edwin C # & 10-9-39, 9-26-43, RM 1/c CRM

Albright, Guy 1-26-45, 3-26-45, S 2/c S 2/c

Alexander, Paul K 11-27-44, 6-1-45, SKD 1/c SKD 1/c

Allen, Dave K & 6-18-41, 5-3-42, SM 2/c SM 2/c

Allen, Lloyd D 7-30-44, 1-2-45, S 1/c S 1/c

Alvey, Harold L 5-27-43, 6-1-45, EM 3/c EH 1/c

Anderson, Donald L 2-7-42, 12-14-44, AS MM 1/c

Anderson, George D 10-28-40, 7-28-41, S 2/c S 1/c Died at Sea

Anderson, Herman W # & 11-1-39, 2-16-42, S 1/c MM 2/c

Archibald, Caster W 7-2-42, 4-13-45, BM 2/c CBM

Arledge, Vernice L 1-16-45, 3-21-45, CMN CMN

Asher, Charles W 11-23-44, 6-1-45, StM 1/c CK 3/c

Ayres, Vern 9-16-43, 11-19-44, SC 3/c SC 2/c

Baird, Clarence W 11-3-44, 3-1-45, S 1/c S 1/c

Baker, William F & 12-2-40, 4-18-43, AS F 2/c

Baldwin, Darrel L 11-3-44, 3-26-45, S 1/c S 1/c

Barfield, Ernest L & 8-7-40, 11-29-43, Cox CBM

Baribeau, Romeo M # & 10-10-39, 9-20-43, F 3/c SC 1/c

Barnes, Clyde H # 10-17-39, 6-3-40, S 1/c Cox

Barney, Royal T 8-17-43, 1-4-45, S 2/c RM 3/c

Barton, Jubilee D 12-27-41, 9-20-43, AS SM 3/c

Baughman, Charles A & 12-2-40, 6-2-42, AS S I/c

Baumbach, Raymond E 5-27-42, 5-14-45, SaM 3/cSoil 3/c

Bechstein, Milton E 8-17-43, 1-31-44, SK 3/c SK 3/c

Bellin, Samuel J 12-2-40, 1-4-41, AS S 2/c

Benfield, John J 1-21-45, 5-14-45, S 2/c QM 3/c

Benton, Paul # & 9-25-39, 11-29-43, OS 2/c CSf (AA)

Berry, Carey W # & 9-25-39, 5-25-42, MM 1/c CMM

Betts, Albers F # 9-25-39, 9-17-41, CM 1/c CM 1/c

Bezzeg, Emery P & 12-2-40, 2-27-43, AS GM 3/c

Biggs, Thomas E # 11-3-39, 6-30-40, YM 3/c YM 2/c

Blachaniec, Edward M 8-17-43, 8-31-43, S 2/c S 2/c

Blackburn, John A 12-27-41, 9-20-43, AS S 1/c

Blaine, James W # & 9-25-39, 5-29-42, AS RM 3/c

Blake, Paul J * 1-26-45, 3-26-45, S 2/c S 2/c

Blakely, Edward N # 9-25-39, 11-4-39, RM 2/c RH 2/c

Blanchard, Marcellus A 8-24-40, 6-25-41, GM 3/c GM 2/c

Blenman, Donald J ??????? 9-18-43, AS ???????

Blythe, Collin V 12-16-44, 5-14-45, F 1/c F 1/c

Borkowski, Richard E 11-3-44, 5-14-45, F 2/c F 1/c

Boudreaux, Ernest J 4-15-43, 6-13-44, Cox BM 1/c
    Died in Sydney from injuries sustained in streetcar accident

Bown, Clifford E 3-22-44, 5-14-45, S 2/c S 1/c

Bracken, Walter C 11-3-44, 6-1-45, S 2/c FCO 3/c

Bradbury, Marvin W & 12-2-40, 1-5-45, AS MM 1/c

Bradley, Howard 2-25-45, 5-14-45, St 3/c St 3/c

Bradshaw, Otis J & 12-30-40, 9-20-43, S 1/c Cox

Bray, Dempster S # 9-30-39, 1-23-40, F 1/c F 1/c

Bremer, Emil A 3-18-40, 6-21-41, Manth 1/c Manth 1/c

Brennan, Thomas F & 12-2-40, 3-25-44, AS S 1/c

Brinkman, Benhard J # 9-25-39, 9-17-41, CMM CMM

Broaddus, Edgar W 12-2-40, 1-4-41, AS S 2/c

Buis, Roy # 10-2-39, 6-11-41, CMM CMM

Bull, William F & 10-14-40, 8-21-43, F 2/c Blmkr 1/c

Bunko, Theodore 10-2-43, 12-14-44, S 2/c GM 2/c

Bunner, Thornton V & 5-1-41, 4-10-43, YM 3/c YM 2/c

Burch, Taft 6-17-43, 12-15-44, S 2/c WT 3/c

Burks, Eugene W & 12-27-41, 7-7-42, AS S 2/c

Burnside, Robert W * 5-13-44, 5-14-45, F 1/c MM 1/c

Buzz, Frank H ????? 3-20-45, SC 1/c CCstd

Caba, Julio # & 9-29-39, 5-26-42, OC 2/c OC 2/c

Caillier, Jules C 12-27-41, 5-14-45, AS WT 1/c

Calhan, Charles L 8-9-43, 6-1-45, RT 2/c RT 1/c

Calkins, Donald L 8-6-43, 5-14-45, S 1/c RM 2/c

Callaway, Ralph P & 6-18-41, 3-4-43, MM 2/c MM 1/c

Campagna, Savadore S 2-1-44, 2-18-45, F 2/c F 1/c Killed In Action

Cardinals, Ceasar J ?????? 11-27-40, F 1/c MM 2/c

Carnevale, James V, Jr. 3-22-44, 12-14-44, S 2/c S 2/c

Caskey, Edwin G # & 9-25-39, 5-26-42, AS QM 3/c

Chapman, Frederic W & 10-9-40, 9-20-43, AS B? 1/c

Christiansen, Carl H & 10-9-40, 5-15-43, AS RM 2/c

Clark, Delbert H 0-26-43, 1-4-44, S 1/c Mn 2/c

Claytor, Richard R 12-27-41, 2-26-44, S 2/c RM 3/c

Clemer, William B 5-27-43, 3-25-44, S 2/c 5 2/c

Cobb, Clifford E & 11-28-40, 5-29-42, S 2/c RM 3/c

Cobb, Paul P & 3-15-40, 3-4-43, AS SF 2/c

Cole, Arzo 11-3-44, 5-14-45, F 2/c F 1/c

Conley, William H # 9-25-39, 5-5-41, F 1/c WT 2/c

Connolly, Richard J ?????? 6-1-45, S 2/c YM 2/c

Constance, Kenneth E 2-1-44, 6-1-45, F 1/c MM 3/c

Cook, Howard E 3-15-40, 1-4-41, AS S 1/c

Cooney, Harold W * 2-1-44, 2-18-45, F 1/c WT 3/c Killed in Action

Cooper, Dale E & 12-2-40, 5-14-45, AS MM 1/c

Cooper, Omar W & 3-15-40, 2-18-43, AS BM 2/c

Cope, John H   10-18-44, 2-19-45,   S 1/c   RM 3/c

Coray, Gene A   #   10-7-39, 3-8-40,   S 1/c   SF 3/c

Corcoran, Robert F   3-10-41, 4-16-41,   SF 3/c   SF 3/c

Cornish, Dawson A   #   9-25-39, 2-26-40,   S 1/c   HA 1/c

Cramer, John J, Jr.   12-2-40, 11-25-41,   AS   S 1/c

Crandall, Donald C   11-3-44, 5-14-45,   S 1/c   S 1/c

Crawford, Edward L   8-24-40, 8-13-41,   GM 3/c   GM 1/c

Crawford, Wilford W   5-10-42, 5-14-45,   S 2/c   GM 1/c

Crisco, Adam   M 8-2-44, 12-15-44,   WT 3/c   WT 3/c

Criss, Acie C   5-10-42, 3-25-44,   S 2/c   RM 3/c

Crouch, James G   3-22-44, 4-15-44,   S 2/c   S 2/c

Cruys, George L   3-16-41, 3-25-41,   AS   AS

Cuda, Joseph V   *   2-1-44, 5-14-45,   F 1/c   MM 3/c

Culley, Paul J   # &   9-25-39, 3-12-43,   MM 1/c   MM 1/c

Cypert, J W   ??????   2-19-45, S 2/c   SM 2/c

Dasch, Joseph M   *   10-18-44, 5-14-45,   S 1/c   SK 3/c

Davis, Fred C   5-13-44, 7-30-44,   St 3/c   St 2/c

Davis, William R   11-17-44, 6-1-45,   S 1/c   SK 3/c

Deblasi, Joseph F   1-16-45, ??????   Mn   2/c

DeFriez, Edwin H   #   9-25-39, 6-29-41,   RM 3/c   RM 1/c

Dettmer, Ellsworth   7-14-42, 5-26-43,   CWT(PA)   CWT(PA)

Diapolo, Ernest J   8-14-43, 2-18-45,   F 2/c   F 2/c   Killed in Action

Dick, Robert A   10-18-44, 6-1-45,   S 1/c   QM 3/c

Dishman, James C   ?????? 6-25-44,   WT 2/c   F 1/c

Dixon, George E   10-2-43, 1-6-44,   S 2/c   S 2/c

Dolan, James C   #   9-25-39, 10-21-41,   S 1/c   RM 3/c

Dorsen, John R   # &   9-25-39, 5-27-42,   EM 1/c   EM 1/c

Doss, Carlos J   #   10-17-39, 3-8-40,   S 1/c GM 3/c

Doubeck, Rudolph   8-17-43, 2-28-45,   S 2/c   BM 2/c

Douglas, Clarence W   # &   9-25-39, 5-15-43,   AS GM 1/c

Dozier, William G # & 10-8-39, 1-12-43,   F 1/c WT 1/c

Duley, Jonny F   2-1-44, 12-14-44,   F 2/c F 1/c

Dunbrasky, Ivan L   2-1-44, 12-22-44,   F 2/c F 1/c

Dwan, Luther # &   8-27-41,11-9-42,   YM 2/c YM 1/c

Easley, Raymond   8-26-43, 12-22-44,   StM 2/c StM 1/c

Edwards, Benjamin F # 9-25-39, 5-13-41,   Cox Cox

Elder, Benjamin C &   12-2-40,   9-20-43,   AS SK 2/c

Elias, Fred J   & 12-2-40, 4-18-43,   AS F 1/c

Ellis, Rolla # &   9-25-39, 2-7-42,   SC 1/c CCStwd

Enderton, Louis E &   6-23-41, ??????   CMM War Mach

Evans, Alfred C #   11-3-39, 6-25-41,   Cox BM 2/c

Fahey, John M & 11-26-41, 7-3-42,   SK 3/c 5K 3/c

Fairhurst, Edward   5-10-42, 11-23-42,   S 2/c S 2/c

Farris, James D # 9-30-39, 5-10-41,   MM 1/c MM 1/c

Fitchpatrick, Curtis B # &   9-25-39, 11-29-44,   Aatt 1/c OS 3/c

Foley, John J # 9-25-39, 7-23-41,   CCStd CCStd

Fonfara. Ralph L   3-16-41, 11-25-41,   AS S 1/c

Fourtner, Kenneth W   1-25-44, 6-1-45,   RM 1/c CRM

Frailly, Gidio A   12-2-40, 12-12-40,   AS AS

Frank, Roger   8-17-42, 5-14-45,   S 2/c QM 2/c

Freedman, Barney   12-2-40, 6-18-41,   AS S 2/c

Freeman, Jacque L   10-26-43, 11-4-43,   GM(M) 1/c GM(M) 1/c

Frisbie, Ross E &   12-26-40, 8-21-43,   F 3/c MM 1/c

Gabbert, Robert H &   3-15-40, 11-29-43,   AS SF 2/c

Garneau, Joseph N   10-16-44, 12-9-44,   SC 3/c SC 3/c

Gates, James W &   12-2-40, 1-31-44,   AS SF 2/c

Gentle, B V & 7-8-41, 11-29-43,   S 2/c SM 2/c

Gentle, J C # &   9-25-39, 7-8-44,   SM 3/cCSM

Gerard, Paul R   5-10-44, 1-2-45,   S 2/c S 1/c

Gilley, Charles A   5-10-42, 9-20-43,   S 2/c S 1/c

Giorgetti, George J   &   12-2-40, 5-14-45,   AS MM 1/c

Haas, John A, Jr.   11-5-43, 11-11-43,   GM(M) 3/c GM(M) 3/c

Hager, Lawrence J 1-26-42, 8-21-43,   AS S 1/c

Hager, Lemuel J 1-26-42, 8-21-43,   AS S 1/c

Hall, James A 1-26-42, 3-4-43,   AS S 1/c

Hambly, Walter H F   # 10-6-39, 6-14-40,   S 1/c QM 3/c

Hamilton, James W, Jr. 5-10-42, 9-20-43,   S 2/c F 1/c

Hamilton, Rex E   8-14-43, 5-14-45,   F 3/c MM 3/c

Haner, Harold V 6-28-40, 11-18-41,   Cox BM 1/c

Hansen, Douglas R 12-27-41, 7-30-44,   AS GM 3/c

Hansen, Richard 5-12-42, 11-29-43,   S 2/c S 1/c

Haralson, Ralph K 1-26-42, 11-29-43,   AS Blmkr 2/c

Harper, Warren R # & 9-25-39, 5-14-44,   AS CMM

Hatherhill, George F # 9-25-39, 10-13-41,   MM 2/c MM 1/c

Hauck, August C # 11-8-39, 6-25-41,   BM 1/c BM 1/c

Haugen, Marlyn G # 10-2-39, 8-14-40,   MM 2/c MM 1/c

Haugen, Marion 0 # & 10-2-39, 9-20-43,   F 1/c WT 1/c

Hauser, Lawrence L 5-27-43, 3-25-44,   5 2/c S 2/c

Hawkins, Robert H   ?????? 3-8-43,   AS S 2/c

Hawkins, David H 1-26-42, 8-16-42,   AS S 2/c

Hawkins, Willis S # 9-25-39, 12-26-39,   S 1/c S 1/c

Haynes, Grover C, Jr. ?????? 6-1-45,   SM   2/c SM 2/c

Hazer, Burnette T, Jr. & 2-25-41, 1-11-42,   AS S 2/c

Heap, Edwin J 1-26-42, 2-18-45,   AS Blmkr 1/c Missing at Sea

Heiges, Sylvester T 8-2-44, 12-12-44,   S 2/c S 2/c

Helms, Ray N 5-12-42, 5-10-43,   S 2/c SoM 3/c

Henderson, John R & 6-7-41, 3-12-43,   QM 3/c QM 3/c

Hendricks, Earl L # & 9-25-39, 10-27-42,   GM   1/c Warr. Gunner

Henry, Patrick A 1-26-42, 5-14-45,   AS MM 1/c

Higgins, William F   ????? 5-14-45,   S 2/c FC 3/c

Hill, Harold W # 9-25-39, 5-10-41, S 1/c F 2/c

Hipp, Alton R ????? 7-30-44, S 2/c S 1/c

Hitzfield, Charles F & 11-23-40, 11-29-43, F 1/c Blmkr 1/c

Hodge, Robert T 1-26-42, 1-20-44, AS S i/c

Hoffman, Donald R & 12-3-40, 3-4-43, AS S 1/c

Holman, Hugh N ????? 5-14-45, F 2/c EM 3/c

Hood, William B 1-26-42, 7-5-42, AS S 2/c

Hopkins, Freddie J 1-26-45, 5-14-45, StM 2/c StM 1/c

Horn, John K # 11-8-39, 4-16-41, MM 1/c MM 1/c

Howard, James W 7-4-42, 1-20-44, AS S 1/c

Howell, Beryl G 1-26-42, 6-24-44, AS SC 1/c

Huddleston, Glenn E & 11-18-41, 5-12-42, 5 2/c S 2/c

Hunter, R.C. 5-10-44, 5-14-45, S 2/c S 1/c

Irysh, David W 5-27-43, 7-8-43, S 2/c 5 2/c

Isham, Lawrence F & 11-18-41, 4-18-43, BM 1/c CBM

Jackson, Alfred L 10-18-44, 3-24-45, S 1/c RM 3/c

Jackson, Horace # & 9-25-39, 9-20-43, WT 2/c CWT

Jackson, William H 5-27-43, 3-20-45, S 2/c SC 1/c

Jacobs, James T 1-26-42, 3-24-44, AS FCM 2/c

Jacobson, William R 5-10-44, 5-14-45, S 2/c S 1/c

James, Olin L # 9-25-39, 10-10-39, CEM CEM

Jarvis, Otis D 12-16-44, 5-15-45, F 1/c F 1/c

Jarvis, Judd M & 12-27-41, 5-14-44, F 3/cMM 1/c

Jaskoba, Phillip & 8-13-41, 5-12-42, CWT CWT

Jeansonn, Norman, Jr 7-2-42, 11-29-43, 2/c SK 3/c

Jensen, Bernard G * 11-3-44, 5-14-45, S 1/c F l/c

Jensen, Paul B 5-13-44, 5-14-45, F 1/c EM 3/c

Jetton, Charles R 1-26-42, 1-20-44, AS EM 3/c

Johns, Charley C ????? 12-2-40, ????? ??????

Johnson, Iver L 8-17-43, 12-14-44, S 2/c S 2/c

Johnson, Marion L 1-26-42, 11-29-43, AS Blmkr 2/c

Jones, Charles C, Jr. 8-24-40, ??????   Ym 3/c ??????

Joos, Donald E 6-15-40, 7-16-40, AS S 2/c

Joos, Harold W & 10-10-40, 1-20-45,   AS CGM(PA)

Judge, Max 0 * 11-3-44, 5-14-45,   S 1/c EM 3/c

Keleman, Frank &   2-4-41, 4-18-43,   Blmkr 2/c Blmkr 1/c

Kelly, Daniel M   ?????? 9-1-44,   AS SC 2/c

Kelly, Ralph G   12-27-41, 5-4-45,   AS EM 3/c

Kemp, Grover C, Jr. 1-26-45, 3-26-45,   S 2/c S1/c

Kemp, Robert D 1-26-42, 6-1-45,   AS CQM

Kemp, William C 1-26-42, ????? AS ?????

Kendrick, Billy J 6-20-43, 3-26-45,   RM 3/c RM 1/c

Kennedy, Dewey A 11-19-43, 11-29-43,   S 1/c S 1/c

Kibbey, Clifford E 8-14-43, 1-2-45,   SoM 3/c SoM 2/c

Kiener, Clemens 1-26-45, 5-14-45,   S 2/c F 2/c

Kingsbury, Clarence J & 6-15-40, 4-18-43,   AS MM 2/c

Kisielewski, Stephen J ????? 5-14-45,   AS SoM 3/c

Knight, Gene E 1-26-45, 3-26-45,   S 2/c S 2/c

Korthe, James C, Jr. # & 10-8-39, 2-27-43,   MM 1/c CMM

Kott, Elmer R & 12-26-40, 7-3-42,   F 3/c F 1/c

Koukos, William L ????? 9-9-43,   AS 5 2/c

Kownacki, Walter 1-21-40, 8-13-40,   AS S 1/c

Kraft, Eugene A   ????? 5-4-45,   F 3/c MM 2/c

Kraner, Robert L 12-27-41, 5-14-45,   AS BM 2/c

Krieger, Jacob L, Jr. & 1-26-41, 1-5-45,   AS WT 2/c

LaForest, Robert B 1-26-42, 3-4-43,   AS S 1/c

Lamb, Stanley H 5-27-43, 12-14-44,   F 2/c Blmkr 3/c

Landes, Garland T, Jr. 1-26-45, 5-14-45,   S 2/c F 2/c

Lang, Roy E # &   9-25-39, 1-7-45,   F 2/c CCstd

LaRocca, Joseph 8-6-43, 5-14-45,   S 1/c RM 3/c

Lathrop, Arthur W & 6-15-40, 4-18-43,   AS SC 2/c

Lathrop, George N 1-16-45, 3-19-45,   Mn 2/c Mn 2/c

LeBlanc, William E # & 9-25-39, 5-26-42, F 1/c MM 1/c

Lee, Newton B 5-27-43, 6-1-45, F 2/c MM 2/c

Lee, Robert A # 9-25-39, 10-3-41, 5 2/c S 1/c

Lentz, Leslie R # & 9-25-39, ????? MM 2/c CMM

LeRoy, Eldon L & 6-15-40, 12-14-44, AS BM 1/c

Leslie, Joseph A 5-27-43, 6-1-45, F 2/c MM 2/c

Lewis, Earnest Jr. 10-2-43, 6-1-45, F 3/c GM 2/c

Lindbeck, Edwin E & 5-10-41, 9-20-43, SF 2/c SF 1/c

Lindell, Sam 2-7-42, 5-12-42, S 1/c S 1/c

Lindsey, James K * 8-14-43, 5-14-45, F 3/c F 1/c

Litz, Edwin H 11-3-44, 2-28-45, S 1/c S 1/c

Lloyd, Garn C 10-2-43, 6-1-45, F 3/c GM 2/c

Lolich, Theodore * 10-18-44, 5-14-45, S 2/c SM 3/c

Lopez, Angelo 1-26-45, 5-14-45, S 2/c S l/c

Lovejoy, Thomas B 8-19-43, 9-26-43, YM 1/c Ym 1/c

Lower, Marvele R 8-14-43, 8-16-44, F 3/c GM 3/c

Lucas, Victor L * 10-18-44, 5-14-45, S1/c RdM 3/c

Luse, Ira R ????? 6-1-45, F 3/c MM 3/c

Luyster, Dean C 3-22-44, 5-14-45, S 2/c S 1/c

Lynch, Leonard E 1-26-45, 3-26-45, S 1/c S 1/c

Machado, Harry W # 9-30-39, 11-7-41, F 2/c F 1/c

MacMillan, Fred S & 10-18-40, 4-18-43, S 2/c F 1/c

Madden, George G 7-22-42, 9-20-43, AS GM 3/c

Madden, John T ????? 6-1-45, F 3/c MM 2/c

Main, Harry A 7-21-42, 6-1-45, AS RdM 2/c

Maiorana, Frank J 11-3-44, 5-14-45, F 3/c F 1/c

Mahoney, Joseph F ????? 1-20-44, F 3/c F 2/c

Mangum, Grover C # 10-8-39, 12-28-39, CEM(PA) CEM(PA)

Manninen, Albert 12-27-41, 2-16-42, S 2/c S2/c

Manning, Zoter Z & 1-21-40, 3-25-44, AS BM 2/c

Marble, William J 8-7-43, 1-1-45, StM 2/c OC 1/c

Marion, Charley 5-22-42, 9-5-43,   MAtt 2/c MA 1/c

Marinage, John C # & 11-3-39, 5-4-42, BM 2/c BM 1/c

Marszalkiewicz, Tony W # 9-2-5-39, 7-19-40, BM 2/c BM 2/c

Martinez, Jaun B 10-16-44, 5-14-45, SC 3/c SC 2/c

Mason, Melvin 8-7-43, 5-22-45, StM 2/c Std 2/c

Masterson, Carl G 2-25-41, 11-12-41, AS S 2/c

Matejicek, Elmer A # 9-25-39, 8-25-41, Ym 3/c YM 1/c

Matysiak, George # 10-14-39, 11-30-39, GM 1/c GM 1/c

Maxwell, Ellsworth A # 9-25-39, 12-21-40, MM 1/c MM 1/c

Maxwell, Fred M # & 9-25-39, 2-20-42, S 1/c Ptr 2/c

Maxwell, Will 0 12-27-41, 2-1-43, S 2/c EM 3/c

Mayfield, Earnest R * 8-7-43, 2-25-45, StM 2/c StM 1/c

McCracken, Walter H & 8-7-40, 7-3-42, QM 2/c QM 1/c

McDonald, Kenneth K 1-4-41, 5-2-41, S 2/c S 2/c

McDonald, Orville D 12-27-41, 9-21-42, AS $ 2/c

McGann, Lyle C * 6-3-43, 5-14-45, S 2/c RdM 3/c

McGuire, George 12-2-40, 12-10-40, CQM(PA) CQM(PA)

McGinley, Nelson A ????? 9-26-43, SK 3/c SK 3/c

McMahon, Charles A # & 9-25-39, 11-9-42, SM 1/c SM 1/c

McPherson, Albert E 2-7-42, 5-26-42, CCStd(PA) CCStd(PA)

Michaud, Lewis ????? 7-9-43, S 1/c S 1/c

Miles, Harold R & 1-21-40, 5-14-45,   AS MM 1/c

Miller, John H 4-15-43, 6-1-45, S 1/c CBM(AA)

Miller, Percey H # 10-8-39, 11-4-39, SM 2/c SM 2/c

Mincher, Llewellyn L # 9-25-39, 10-19-40, SC 3/c SC 3/c

Mitchell, Floyd 12-2-44, 12-14-44, 5 2/c S 2/c

Mitchell, John C # 10-8-39, 11-22-40, F 2/c F 1/c

Montecalvo, Frank & 10-9-40, 5-1-44, AS MM 2/c

Moors, Mark J' # & 9-25-39, 9-20-43, CGM(PA) CGM(PA)

Morgan, Robert 2-7-42, 8-21-43, S 1/c F 1/c

Morgison, LeRoy E 10-2-43, 5-14-45, F 3/c F 1/c

Moss, Rufus M # 9-25-39, 10-16-39, CWT(PA) CWT(PA)

Mullin, Elmer B # 9-25-39, 5-3-42, CQM(PA) CQM(PA)

Murvin, James L 8-6-43, 6-1-45, EM 3/c EM 2/c

Myers, Harvey C 1-21-40, 7-19-40, AS S 2/c

Nasworthy, John P 2-27-44, 12-15-44, SK 3/c SK 3/c

Neely, Frank # & 2-5-39, 11-9-42, MAtt 2/c OS 2/c

Neer, Francis J 1-26-45, 3-26-45, S 2/c S 2/c

Nelson, Gayle W & 1-4-41, 1-11-42, S 1/c GM 3/c

Newman, Lester C # 10-9-39, 4-18-40, F 1/c F 1/c

Nicholas, Edward S # 9-27-39, 12-21-40, F 2/c MM 2/c

Niederhaus, Emmanuel 5-27-43, 5-14-45, F 2/c M41, 2/c

Nightingale, David W # 9-27-39, 8-25-41, F 2/c F 1/c

Noble, Thomas E 1-16-45, 5-14-45, F 2/c F 1/c

Nolan, Joseph R & 4-5-41, ????? RM 3/c RM 1/c

Nolan, Kenneth G & 4-5-41, 5-2-42, RM 3/c RM 3/c

North, Carl M 1-31-44, 9-5-44, CPhmM(AA) CPhM(AA)

Notter, Alvan C # & 9-29-39, 1-23-44, AS GM 1/c

Noyes, Otis W # & 9-25-39, 9-20-43, QM 2/c CQM(PA)

Noyes, Thomas L 8-2-44, 5-14-45, S 1/c GM 3/c

Nunal, Pio # 10-8-39, 10-18-39, OS 2/c OS 2/c

Nunnally, Ebbert 9-18-43, 5-14-45, SoM 3/c SaM 3/c

Olhson, Carl G 10-18-44, 5-14-45, F 1/c EM 3/c

Olson, Richard E 10-2-43, 6-1-45, F 3/c WT 3/c

Ortiz, Carmel Z 10-2-43, 6-1-45, F 3/c F 1/c

Parker, James D 12-2-40, 11-22-41, AS S 1/c

Peak, Joseph C # 10-14-39, 1-1-39, S 1/c S 1/c

Pearl, Gerald G # 11-1-39, 5-21-40, YM 3/c YM 3/c

Peasley, Douglas G & 10-18-40, 1-27-42, S 2/c F 2/c

Peck, Leo A 5-13-44, 5-14-45, CM 3/c CM 3/c

Pells, Robert T # 10-2-39, 1-25-41, WT 2/c WT 2/c

Pepper, Keith E & 3-15-40, 1-20-44, AS EM 1/c

Phillips, John H   12-27-41, 6-24-44,   AS RM 2/c

Pickerhill, Arnold L   10-2-43, 6-1-45,   F 3/c MM 3/c

Pietrowski, Donald J &   3-6-40, 7-30-44,   SM 3/c SM 1/c

Piper, Floyd S # &   9-25-39, 4-18-43,   EM 3/c CEM(AA)

Pitts, Sterling, J H   3-22-44, 6-1-45,   S 2/c S 1/c

Posey, Reginald H 4-29-44, 5-14-45,   S 1/c S 1/c

Potacki, George A # &   9-25-39, 5-16-43,   CBM(PA) Warr Bo'sn

Present, Manuel   1-26-45, 3-2.6-45,   S 2/c S 2/c

Prokop, Joseph   3-22-44, 2-28-45,   S 2/c SK 3/c

Pyles, Eldridge   8-2-44, 3-26-45,   F 1/c S 1/c

Ramsey, Wilks &   10-29-41, 7-14-42,   CMM(PA) CMM(PA)

Rankin, Milton I   9-7-44, 6-1-45,   S 2/c S 1/c

Rehder, Vernon H &   6-15-40, 6-24-44,   AS GM 1/c

Replogle, Raymond J   7-22-42, 2-14-45,   AS SF 2/c

Reynolds, Franklin D   9-25-39,   5-15-45,   F 2/c CEM(PA)

Reynosa, Edward L   7-30-44, 6-1-45,   YM 2/c YM 2/c

Rice, Wilson # &   9-25-39, 5-14-45,   AS CMM(PA)

Richardson, Shirley W   1-19-42, ??????   CPhM(AA) CPhM(PA)

Richmond, Ray P # &   10-8-39, 1-30-42,   F 3/c F 2/c

Riley, Stewart W &   11-30-40, 5-29-42,   AS 5 2/c

Roachell, James M #   0-16-39, 11-27-41,   CWT(PA) CWT(PA)

Robe, Glenn   2-21-40, 8-7-41,   AS 5K 3/c

Roberts, Jefferson D &   10-8-40, 12-14-44,   AS SF 2/c

Roberts, William L # &   9-25-39, 5-26-42,   S 1/c BM 2/c

Robertson, J W   10-13-44, ??????   YM 3/c ??????

Rodgers, Theodore G   ?????? 12-14-44, S 2/c YM 2/c

Rogers, Reece Aerial # &   9-25-39, 5-14-44,   F 2/c CWT(AA)

Rogers, Rodney W   9-7-44, 12-15-44,   S 2/c S 2/c

Runion, Charles A #   9-25-39, 4-7-41,   F 1/c MM 2/c

Russell, Richard W &   11-20-40, 5-14-44,   AS WT 1/c

Salfer, Frank A, Jr. 7-20-44, 5-14-45, F 2/c F 1/c

Salvail, Charles A 9-18-43, 5-14-45, S 2/c RdM 3/c

Sanchez, Eley L 8-2-44, 5-14-45, S 2/c F 2/c

Sapp, Clayton R 10-18-40, 11-18-40, F 1/c F 1/c

Schwarzhoff, William T, Jr. & 1-4-41, 1-11-42, GM 2/c GM 1/c

Schwieder, Robert M & 2-25-41, 1-11-42, AS S 1/c

Schutz, Albert F ?????? 2-18-45, WT 2/c WT 2/c Killed in Action

Selen, Alden A # 9-2-5-39, 4-1-40, Msmth 1/c Msmth 1/c

Seymour, Alfred 3 # 9-30-39, 8-14-40, F 1/c F 1/c

Sharp, Theodore A # 10-8-39, ?????? WT 2/c ??????

Shepard, Charles 9-18-43, 6-1-45, S 2/c RdM 2/c

Shogan, Julius L 1-15-45, 6-1-45, SC(B) 2/c SC(B) 1/c

Skinner, Richard H & 1-8-40, 4-13-44, AS MM 1/c

Skinner, William # & 9-27-39, 5-9-43, F 2/c MM 1/c

Slaughter, Clyde E & 11-28-40, 9-20-43, AS FC 2/c

Slaughter, Hyrum B 12-27-41, 5-29-42, S 2/c S 1/c

Slocum, Charles M # & 9-25-39, 9-20-43, F 3/c MM 2/c

Slusser, Charles D 12-16-44, 1-7-45, F 2/c F 2/c

Smith, Audis I 9-7-44, 3-26-45, S 2/c S2/c

Smith, Charles G & 9-19-41, 1-20-44, S 2/c YM 2/c

Smith, Kermit # 9-30-39, 6-3-40, BM 1/c BM 1/c

Smith, Lloyd Thomas 12-2-40, 12-10-40, BM 2/c 8M 2/c

Smith, Robert G 6-29-42, 12-14-44, F 3/c5 1/c

Smithart, Alton C # & 10-9-39, 1-29-42, WT 1/c WT 1/c

Soehnge, Herbert H 9-25-39, 10-4-39, AS AS

Souligny, Eugene W 9-25-39, 12-13-40, MM 2/c MM 1/c

Springfield, Hunt A 8-2-44, 12-10-44, YM 3/c YM 2/c

Spurgeon, Lee F 1-16-45, 5-14-45, Mn 1/c Mn 1/c

Standridge, Woodrow W # & 9-25-39, 5-9-43, F 1/c WT 1/c

Starr, Melvin C # 9-25-39, 9-3-40, S 1/c S 1/c

Starring, Charles E 3-22-44, 5-14-45, F 1/c MM 3/c

Stefanick, Francis   ?????? 12-14-44,   F 3/c S i/c

Stewart, Douglas H   8-2-44, 6-1-45,   F 1/c SF 3/c

Strom, Orvin M   3-22-43, 4-16-45,   F 1/c MM 3/c

Sturak, John 7-22-42, 7-25-42,   AS AS Left at Palmyra Island Hospital

Styles, Andrew # &   9-25-39, 7-9-43,   MAtt 3/c MAtt 1/c

Sullivan, John W   10-2-43, 6-1-45,   F 2/c MM 2/c

Summers, Virgil R   11-3-44, 5-14-45,   F 2/c F I/c

Tadeusiak, Theodore H   10-2-43, ??????   F 2/c F 1/c

Talley, Forest L   1-16-45, 5-14-45,   RT 3/c RT 2/c

Tatum, James V   12-16-44, 6-1-45,   StM 2/c StM 1/c

Taylor, Jay W   ?????? 3-5-43,   F 3/c F 3/c

Taylor, Robert L   7-2-42, 11-27-43,   WT 2/c WT 1/c

Thomas, Wilbut G   9-3-44, ??????   S 2/c CPhM(AA)

Thompson, Bernice C # &   11-1-39, 2-16-42,   EM 2/c EM 1/c

Thompson, James R #   10-6-39, 2-4-41,   F 3/c F 1/c

Tomlin, Clarence 0 &   1-4-41, 3-25-44,   GM 2/c GM 1/c

Torrey, Carl C & 9-19-41, 5-14-45,   S 2/c MM 1/c

Toth, Stephan J # &   9-25-39, 12-14-44,   F 1/c CMM(AA)

Trice, Clyde L # &   9-25-39, 12-30-42,   FC 2/c FC 1/c

Trujillo, Euard #   9-25-39, 11-14-40,   WT 1/c WT 1/c

Trujillo, Gilbert A   11-19-43, 11-29-43,   GM(M) 2/c GM(M) 2/c

Urban, Albert W # &   9-29-39, 1-26-42,   PhM 1/c CPhM(AA)

VanDerVells, Phillip M   ?????? 12-15-44,   AS GM 3/c

Van Metre, Byron   11-11-43, ??????   Officer - rank unk.

Van Nauker, Jack R E ?????? 1-20-44,   F 3/c F 1/c

Vaultrot, Leonard   12-2-40, 12-10-40,   CSM(PA) CSM(PA)

Ventura, Florencio # &   10-18-39, 5-14-44,   MAtt 1/c Ck 2/c

Vernon, John M, Jr.   7-21-42, 5-14-45,   AS WT 2/c

Vick, Elbert L, Jr. &   11-28-40, 1-11-42,   AS S 2/c

Vogel, William E, Jr. &   11-28-40, 1-11-42,   AS S 1/c

Voyles, Maurice R &   11-28-40, 1-7-45,   AS GM 1/c

Wade, Charles F   8-6-43, 2-19-45,   S 2/c SK 2/c

Walker, Chesley 0   3-22-44, 3-26-45,   S 2/c S 1/c

Walker, Norman W #   9-25-39, 8-16-40,   AS F 2/c

Walkup, Biford G #   10-2-39, 6-15-40,   Blmkr 1/c Blmkr 1/c

Ward, Edward P   *   10-19-44, 6-1-45,   S 2/c SoM 3/c

Watson, Ralph C. Jr. # &   9-25-39, ???????   CRM(PA) Warr. Elect.

Wheeler, Wayne B   7-21-42, 9-16-43,   SC 2/c SC 1/c

Whiting, Walter J   ?????? 9-20-43,   F 2/c F 2/c

Whitney, William R #   9-25-39, 11-11-41,   SK 2/c SK 1/c

Wiggins, Herbert W   7-2-42, 5-19-44,   S 2/c YM 2/c

Wigginton, LeRoy   10-18-44, 2-19-45,   S 1/c RM 3/c

Wilcox, David R   7-2-42, 5-14-45,   S 2/c BM 1/c

Willard, Merral A   ?????? 3-25-44,   SK 3/c SK 3/c

Williams, Alfred J   9-16-43, 5-14-45,   S 2/c 5 1/c

Williams, Edgar H   9-16-43,6-1-45,   S 2/c Cox

Williams, Jack R   9-16-43, 3-26-45,   S 2/c S 1/c

Williams, Paul M   9-16-43, 6-1-45,   S 2/c GM 3/c

Williams, William P   9-16-43, 11-28-44,   S 2/c S 2/c

Williamson, Felix H, Jr.   ?????? 12-20-44,   F 2/c WT 2/c

Wilmot, Donald D   9-16-43, 12-8-44,   S 2/c SC 3/c

Wilson, Ronald W   ?????? 6-25-44,   MM 2/c F 1/c

Wingard, Merrill D   1-25-45, 3-26-45,   S 2/c S 2/c

Winsley, Jack R   9-16-43, 10-6-44,   S 2/c S i/c

Winters, David B   9-16-43, 12-14-44,   S 2/c S 1/c

Wisdom, Hilary E   9-16-43, 12-14-44,   S 2/c S 2/c

Wittneben, Henry L *   9-16-43, 5-14-45,   S 2/c GM 3/c

Wofford, Jimmie C   ?????? 2-28-45,   S 2/c Cox

Wolfenbarger, Herbert   7-2-42, 11-4-42,   S 2/c S 2/c

Woodward, Robert K   7-21-42, 11-29-43,   AS S 1/c

Work, Samuel B   8-2-44, 5-14-45,   S 2/c S l/c

Wray, Paul L #   10-8-39, 10-18-39,   OC 2/c OC 2/c

Wright, George W A   11-5-43, 11-11-43,   GM(M) 1/c GM(M) 1/c

Yarbrough, James W *   7-2-42, 5-14-45,   WT 2/c CWT(PA)

Youens, William H #   9-25-39, 5-4-42,   YM 1/c CYM(AA)

Young, Ernest E *   7-2-42, 5-14-45,   S 2/c GM 2/c

Three men were on GAMBLE from the day it was re-commissioned through the bombing at Iwo Jima:

Adams, Charles W AS to CMM

Reynolds, Franklin D F 2/c to CEM(PA)

Rice, Wilson AS to CIWI(PA)

Two others were on almost as long:

Lang, Roy E off 1-7-45,   F 2/c to CCstd

Toth, Stephan J off 12-14-44, F 1/c to CMM(AA)

C. G. Smith's Story

After high school in 1937, I returned to New Jersey to find work and start out in the world. I went to Newark, New Jersey and worked several jobs for about six months and finally found a job in the sales department of a paper cup manufacturer, the Mono Service Company. I worked there for about three years.

This was the late thirties when jobs were scarce. I thought I was on my way, earning $18 a week. My room rent was a whopping $3 a week. A weekly dining card at Bill's Diner was $5, leaving $10 to splurge. The work was interesting and I liked the people and it gave me hope that it could build into something better. In one year I got a raise to $24.

My buddy, Ed Broadwell, had a car and we had great times in New Jersey. Mom had left Maine and was working as a nurse in Brooklyn, New York. My sister, Elinor, had married Frank Richmond and lived in Huntington, Long Island. Mom had decided to let Dorothy, my youngest sister, live with my Aunt Dot in Long Branch and finish her high school there. It was nice that we were all located close enough to visit and we got together frequently.

Those days the big events were the weekends when we got our dates together, pooled our money and scouted where the big bands were playing. The most famous place for me was Frank Daley's Meadowbrook in northern New Jersey. Many times we went there and enjoyed shows featuring Tommy Dorsey and his band and listened to the hottest young vocalist, Frank Sinatra. The comedian who kept us in stitches was Jackie Gleason. All this for about ten bucks apiece. How could you beat it? Another spot I liked was The Pink Elephant; the singer there was Tony Martin.

Things were changing every day or so it seemed, and war was threatening in Germany and creating a lot of anxiety throughout the world. Our country was anticipating a crisis to the extent that they passed a draft act to beef up our meager armed forces. They assigned each participant a number and then called on them to serve as their number appeared. My number mandated my joining the service within three months. I beat them to the punch and joined the Navy in February, 1941. I completed boot training in Newport, Rhode Island, and was sent to a training school in San Diego. I completed a course as a radioman, and was shuttled off to Hawaii for assignment in the Pacific Fleet.

I reported on board the USS GAMBLE in September of 1941, and here began a great episode of my life. The "G," as we called her, was a 1918 four stack destroyer that had been converted to a high speed minelayer. If you have ever read the story of the Caine mutiny, you will recall a vivid description of a crew and ship that would equally describe the G, my home for two and a half years.

She was beat up, ugly, and held together by luck and the dedication of a tough bunch of guys who cursed about everything connected with her, but were proud to be counted as members of her crew.

Our mine division always anchored off the Pearl City pier not far from where the Clipper sea planes landed going to the Far East. This was peacetime, and other than routine operations around the islands, we were usually at anchor and free for liberty on the weekends. I was a first class seaman making little money and usually broke, but I managed to get ashore whenever the opportunity presented itself. I had great times in Honolulu, Pearl City, and the many other areas in the islands.

On December 7, 1941, I had the duty and was on board without half of our normal crew. Many crew members were married an spent the nights ashore. After reveille, about 6 am, I attended to my regular duties which included cleaning up the well deck area. This began at the call "Clean sweep down fore and aft." This accomplished, I was enjoying a cup of coffee and shooting the breeze with a radioman named Cobb when we heard the first earthshaking explosion. We both thought that a plane had crashed on Ford Island, and we were not overly excited.

Further explosions and huge billows of smoke and flames from the Ford Island area soon convinced us that something big was happening. Lt. Bogart, senior officer in command, shouted from the bridge that it was an air attack by the Japanese. The ship's PA sent us to our battle stations. Guys were yelling, awnings were being ripped down, and I stood by my battle station as a 5-inch gun loader.

Our gun crew was sent forward to break out ammo for the AA guns on the bridge. I believe I witnessed one of the war's first kamikaze actions when a Jap plane crashed into the stern of the USS CURTIS, berthed next to us. For half an hour, it was a series of doing what was needed, and finally we had to steam up and get under way. The harbor was a mess, small craft running all over the place— including our motor whale boat which had been sent to pick up our skipper. It returned with him making a neat Chinese gangway.

Word was passed that a small Jap sub was in the harbor, and we took after it. I don't know if it was really there or not, but we dropped about three depth charges adjacent to the carrier berths that shook the hell out of us if not them. We were ordered out of harbor and proceeded to do so but were stalled when the NEVADA obstructed the passage out. She was sinking. Luckily, she stayed afloat long enough to back down into a canebrake. We steamed out to take up patrol and screen carriers due in.

After the big day, our squadron was ordered to mine the unconquered islands in the South Pacific. This took us to Pago Pago, the Fiji Islands, New Guinea, New Caledonia, the Hebrides, the Solomons, the Philippines, and Australia.

I was aboard the GAMBLE until 1943 when I was sent back to the US for new construction, outfitting and commissioning a new ship in the Admiralty Islands, a CVE (small carrier). I returned to the South Pacific on this ship until the war's end in 1945. I transferred to the USS SARATOGA, engaged in returning troops to the US. Having had a long period of sea duty, I was eligible and applied for shore duty, being assigned to duty in the Bureau of Naval Personnel, Washington, DC. That was in 1946.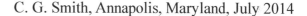

C. G. Smith, Annapolis, Maryland, July 2014

Left to Right: C. G. Smith, Shorty Gentile, and J. D. Roberts. Taken at the Silver Rail on Market Street in San Francisco, California on September 15, 1943.

14122557R00066